TROPICAL FISH

Keeping Journal

Book Edition Four

Written by Alastair R Agutter

For the Dedicated Aquarist and Tropical Fish Hobbyist World Wide

Tropical Fish Keeping Journal

Book Edition Four

Written, Designed and Created by

Alastair R Agutter (Author)

www.alastairagutter.com

Cover and Inside Book Photograph by

Alastair R Agutter

Cover Picture: Super Foods

High Protein Beef Heart Foods for Tropical Fish and Discus

Published by Create Space Independent
An Amazon Group Company

Printed, Sold and Distributed by
Amazon and other Reputable Book
Stores and Wholesalers World-Wide
www.amazon.com

1st Edition Published 7th September 2017

Available in Traditional Print and Digital

ISBN-13: 978-1976140587

ISBN-10: 1976140587

Table of Contents:

Introduction

Dear Reader and Aquarist,

Firstly, a very big welcome to the **"Tropical Fish Keeping Journal"** and a special thank you for acquiring this copy of the publication **"edition four"** in the series. I must apologise for the delay in this issue, but unfortunately at the end of April this year in 2017 I had heart failure. But as they say now, I keep on taking the tablets and I am slowly on the mend.

Copyright © Photograph by Alastair R Agutter

Aquarists Diary & News

Whilst recovering from poor health recently, it has given me an opportunity to look at the Tropical Fish scene on the World Wide Web. A few years back, the interest online was very much in decline. I noted then, many tropical fish keeping web sites and forums, were either shutting down, or simply not being updated.

Tropical Fish Keeping Social Networking

Today however, I am pleased to see a resurgence of interest again across the World Wide Web. This is very heartening, especially on the Social Media Networks scene, where there are some fantastic groups and sites appearing. One I have been particularly taken with recently has been an aquatic landscaping site, by Oliver Knott. Oliver today, appears to be a leading designer in the field of aquatics, with some spectacular aquatic underwater scenes created. I urge any aquarist, experienced, or new to our hobby, to take a look, for I am sure Oliver's web site will truly inspire. The web site address is: http://www.oliver-knott.com/

Oliver Knott with one of his Massive Aquascape Creations in Germany

If you are a Facebook user and fan, and can't get enough of Social Networking, Oliver has a web site and pages on the platform also, displaying some of his amazing creations. The Facebook web site address is: https://www.facebook.com/pg/okaqua/

Another web site worth visiting online is at Facebook and ran by Ibrahim Erkanat known as Discus and Angel Fish. Some of the images of the fish species including videos are remarkable. As I look at these vibrant heavy set coloured species, it clearly demonstrates how far we have come, since my early days of breeding Wild Discus. Ibrahim's Facebook address is: https://www.facebook.com/ibrahim.erkanat

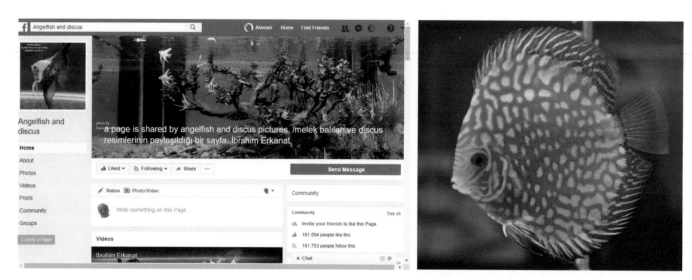

Visit the Very Popular Facebook Discus and Angel Fish Web Site by Ibrahim Erkanat

Above is a fine example of a European Tank Bred Discus of many generations to attain these colours. Distant Wild relatives of this species, would of involved the cross breeding of the symphysodon aequifasciata haraldi (Blue Discus) and the symphysodon aequifasciata axelrodi (Brown Discus).

Tropical Fish Super Foods

In this issue of the Tropical Fish Keeping Journal I feature one of my most recent tropical fish books written this year in 2017, titled "Super Foods Tropical Fish and Discus", covering the great importance and the many benefits to making your own high protein super foods for healthy, thriving, disease free, tropical fish species.

Feeding Tropical Fish

In this feature of the Tropical Fish Keeping Journal, provides great advice on feeding your tropical fish, and the amount of food to give your charges. Over the years also, I have seen many tropical fish foods sold to the aquarist, some are beneficial and some can be very detrimental to your tropical fish. I hope this feature puts all tropical fish hobbyists on the right path for life.

Aquarists Fish Care and Maintenance

Routine checks and maintenance to your aquarium, is one of the great secrets to the successful keeping of your tropical fish. We very often read about setting up an aquarium, and what types of tropical fish we can keep. But do we ever really hear, or read, articles about the actual maintenance and after care regarding our hobby and pastime. This feature in the Tropical Fish Keeping Journal provides practical advice and guidance.

Tropical Fish Species

In every issue of the Tropical Fish Keeping Journals, I like to cover and introduce to new aquarists, specific species of tropical fish with fact files that do include their genealogy and ancestry.

Aquatic Plant Species

In every issue of the Tropical Fish Keeping Journals, I also have an "Editor's Choice" featuring and introducing a selection of aquatic plant species for new and existing aquarists, accompanied with fact files of each species. I fondly recall how important I found such material as a young boy learning about our pastime. Such features very often covered in the very early editions of the Tropical Fish Hobbyist Magazine, by my friend and yours Herbert Axelrod.

Aquarists Products Guide

New and existing reliable Products and Equipment, is obviously very important for our pastime. Especially regarding the well-being and care of live marine creatures, and completely dependent on our due diligence as dedicated aquarists.

Aquarists Reference Tables

Over the years, I have designed and created many tables to help aquarists, regarding water quality, volume mass of water, actual gallons, or litres for specific sized aquariums etc. Here are more great tables, along with more mathematical calculations and formulas in some instances, to help all aquarists and tropical fish hobbyists.

New and Future Tropical Fish Keeping Journal Book Editions Numbers Four to Nine

Aquarists Book Guide

Again in this issue of the Tropical Fish Keeping Journal are more reviews concerning great essential books and magazines worth reading to acquire, covering our time honoured and noble traditional pastime of tropical fish keeping.

Aquarists Directory

Lastly in this issue but not least, Tropical Fish Keeping Journal Edition Four, covers and lists more useful online resources and web site addresses, for aquarists new and experienced of all ages, in relation to more products and equipment

What's coming in future issues.......

Future Tropical Fish Keeping Journal Book Edition Ten - My First Aquarium Book Celebrating 50 years for every Aquarist and Super Foods Tropical Fish and Discus Book – All out and on sale Now!

Tropical Fish Keeping Journal Book Edition Five

In book edition five of the **"Tropical Fish Keeping Journal"** we cover; cures and remedies for fish diseases and with the avoidance of chemicals, to a specially prepared and created set of aquarists reference tables detailing aquarium sizes, filtration rates, heating requirements and sizes for aquariums, lighting wattage for fish tanks, biological culture volume mass, conversions and mathematical formulas for aquariums in litres, imperial US gallons and UK gallons, to identifying the different methods and techniques, surrounding tropical fish reproduction (breeding).

Tropical Fish Keeping Journal Book Edition Six

In book edition six of the **"Tropical Fish Keeping Journal"** we cover; essential equipment and worthwhile practical products, how to become a DIY aquarist and to start utilizing household items for the family aquarium or fish house, to making your own all glass aquarium, making a filtration system, the aquarists products directory to the useful book reads guide.

Tropical Fish Keeping Journal Book Edition Seven

In book edition seven of the **"Tropical Fish Keeping Journal"** we cover; essential equipment and worthwhile practical products, how to become a DIY aquarist and to start utilizing household items for the family aquarium or fish house, to making your own all glass aquarium, making a filtration system, the aquarists products directory to the useful book reads guide.

Much more to come.......

God Bless, Sincere Best Wishes to All,

Alastair R Agutter

Aquarist and Author

Tropical Fish Super Foods

Last year, when making up more **"Super Foods"** for my Discus and other Tropical Fish I keep and breed. It suddenly struck me, how helpful and important it would be to share my recipes with all other members of the tropical fish keeping community world-wide.

I then remembered a line from one of my favourite films, We Bought a Zoo, and where in the film, the beautiful Scarlet Johannsson, asked Mat Damon the main star of the film "why did he buy a zoo!" To which his reply was, "why not!"

It Was Fate.........

At around about the same time, while making more Super Foods, for my Discus and Tropical Fish, I was starting to run out of ideas on what to eat myself. I didn't realize at the time I was in such poor health, as my condition of deterioration was a gradual thing, and I put my breathing difficulties down to air pollution, not heart failure later! So to get some ideas and to cheer myself up, I started trawling the net for Food Books, as you do!

Jamie Oliver Left Famous Chef, Nigella Lawson Centre Food Goddess, lastly Matt Damon and Scarlett Johansson in the Movie We Bought a Zoo

First port of call planned was Jamie, of Jamie Oliver Naked Chef Fame, and after that of course the Brunette Goddess of Cooking, Nigella Lawson. But my first port of call to Jamie was very fortuitous, for there on display, on the home page of his web site, showed a picture of his new book titled "Super Foods", of course this book was for us humans. But it got me thinking again.

If I recall, it was the following day I felt a lot better in myself with some milder weather, when I began to start planning out and writing "Super Foods Tropical Fish and Discus" as a book, the rest is history as they say in the movies!

How Super Foods Benefit You, Your Discus, and Other Tropical Fish Species

Going back to the 1970's and 1980's, when trying to breed Wild Discus, in truth I was struggling at first. So never think anything is ever easy if you are a young aquarist reading this, life can be tough, and you just have to keep on trying!

So all that I had read about Discus and trying to breed them, I decided to tear up and forget. So for several days I put my thinking cap on, and started to look at things from a different angle. I in fact tried to put myself in the minds and position of the fish, thinking what would I want in the way of conditions to be content and want to procreate.

Back in the 1980's, it soon become apparent to me, that one thing we do all like as a form of security in our lives, is routine! The food at the same time, I was feeding my Discus Fish, consisted of some live foods, frozen bloodworms, krill, and lobster eggs. Feeding times for my fish seemed to be a reluctant necessity, there was never any real enthusiasm, and disease ailments continued as a regular thing.

Left hand feeding my Discus with one of the Super Food Recipes, Centre Angel Fish Spawning on a Diet of Super Foods, lastly a Breeding Pair of Pseudotropheus *in full condition*

My Wild Discus even after acclimatization, never really seemed to put any weight on, I knew when having such honest questions asked of myself, this was the road to nowhere, with regards to breeding these majestic fish species.

One contact I knew who was also a Cichlid Keeper, but always reluctant to give any advice and very often talked in riddles, mentioned the word "Beef Heart" one time, during the course of another senseless conversation. This got me thinking, and so I looked into what Jack (Jack Wattley) was doing, and "The Doctor" (Dr. Eduard Schmidt-Focke) with regards to food and diets.

I thought to myself at the time, to hell with it, I will go full throttle at this, I have nothing to lose and going to do this my way, with regards to food, water, and filtration!

So the very first thing I done, was to design and build a totally new concept in filtration, a system we know today as "Trickle Filtration" and powered by the most powerful powerhead I could find at the time. I set this filtration system up in one of my main aquariums, a fish tank that was naturally planted, and housing a number of my large, and rare adult Wild Discus.

I researched and looked into the protein and minerals found in the Wild where the Discus lived in their natural habitat, this being in South America, the River Amazon and other Rivers in the region. With the first batch of Beef Heart I made, I included a number of other ingredients that contained the same proteins and minerals found in the Wild.

I then started to acclimatize my fish to my local tap water supply, so I had an abundance of water for my Discus on tap as they say!

I was amazed, with the regular water changes and the new feeding regime, how my Discus reacted to the new super food and conditions. At every feeding time, my Discus frantically ate the new food, and after a few weeks, I could see my Discus putting on weight, growing in size and starting to pair off!

I also started to notice and realize that my Discus's ailments and diseases contracted by my fish were decreasing by the day. I also realized and noticed also from my study, and since those times, that most diseases are caused from stress, and mostly related to poor diet.

Here below is one of my recipes found in my new book for you to try. All the ingredients can be regularly and easily obtained from your local Grocers, Supermarket and Butchers.

Beef Heart and Liver – Suitable for both adult and young fish

You will require:-

4 lbs Fresh Beef Heart

4 oz. Fresh Liver

1 Multi-Vitamin tablet

3 Tablespoons Vegetable Flake Food

1/2lb Fresh Spinach

1 Sachet of Gelatine

Recipe Instructions

First you need to find yourself a good sized glass bowl, and then you need a liquidiser that has the ability to grind coffee. Put the beef heart on to a chopping board and cut away the fat and valves of the heart, leaving only the meat, which should be cut into small cubes. Place the chopped meat into the liquidiser, using the coffee grind setting, and then grind for a few times, until almost pasty. Continue to do the same with all the beef heart, then put into the glass bowl.

Cut the liver into cubes, but add this straight to the bowl with the tablespoons of flaked food. Using warm water, dissolve the vitamin tablet and mix in all the ingredients. Chop the spinach into fine species, liquidise them and add to the other ingredients, mixing well. Finally take one sachet of gelatine and about one inch of water or one cup and add to a milk size saucepan; heat gently and mix in the gelatine until it becomes slightly pasty, then stir the gelatine into the ingredients and mix vigorously to ensure it has been blended in thoroughly. Finally, packing for the freezer is done easily, by way of open freezing, where you spread the mixture on a baking tray to make squares or rectangles, whichever is preferable, to permit easy separation once frozen for freezer bags. I always use this process when freezing down all these recipes I use for my fish.

Feeding Tropical Fish

The second most important aspect to tropical fish keeping after great aquarium water conditions is without doubt food.

Photograph above showing some high protein fresh fish food being made using one of the Author's Recipes – Photograph by Alastair R Agutter

The above photograph shows how as a tropical fish hobbyist and aquarist you can in fact make your own high protein tropical fish food and on the following pages as we discuss fish food are some recipes to try.

I became inspired to create my own fish food to compliment others we can all obtain from tropical fish shop retailers or online today, was when trying to breed Wild Discus (symphysodon) in captivity, for these poor souls being flown in from South America and arriving to me were terribly thin and run down, literally on death's door!

One thing we all learn as Aquarists as the years pass by on our continued journey of tropical fish keeping, is if we want to breed our fish successfully in captivity, we need to bring our tropical fish into a healthy breeding condition and this can only be achieved by providing the right food and conditions, so those very special magical days finally arrive, where your fish reward you for all your hard work and efforts by spawning.

Admittedly, some tropical fish species are prolific breeders, such as Guppies and Platies. But even with these fish species, by providing a balanced and healthy high protein fish food diet, this will see guppies and platies growing to a much larger size and producing far more off-spring.

Many ah Clubs Aquarist of old visiting another member, can always provide an experience and story surrounding fish food, water and breeding. Such dedication is like the Leek, or Marrow grower in prize gardening, and if you are lucky enough to be invited into their World, you become blown away from their vegetable growing results and in our case regarding their tropical fish keeping exploits and charges.

In the 1960's and 1970's, I was fortunate enough to experience some of those memorable golden moments when visiting other aquarists. Such special moments and fond memories in tropical fish keeping that will last and stay with me the rest of my life and for all eternity. The sight of Guppies and Platies in their tens of thousands, Neon and Cardinal Tetra's being bred successfully amongst horse hair in old slowly leaking and rusting angle iron aquariums, to Discus fish the size and diameter of dinner plates, are cherished moments that can never be forgot.

So let's take a detailed look at tropical fish foods, so you can too hopefully become successful like those memorable aquarists I have had the pleasure to know in the past!

Regarding tropical fish food there are essentially four general types and these are 1/. Flake Foods, 2/. Live Foods, 3/. Frozen Foods and 4/. Pellet and Freeze Dried Foods.

For today's aquarists, over the years the diversity and makes available in tropical fish foods has forever increased. Today's Tropical Fish Hobbyists and Aquarists are very much spoilt for choice and sometimes it can become a little confusing.

So I hope the way I have set out the details of fish foods in this chapter sheds some light on the subject and greatly helps.

Flake Fish Foods

Over the years, three of the main staple diet flake foods that can be readily obtained from retail tropical fish stores are; King British, Aquarian and Tetra.

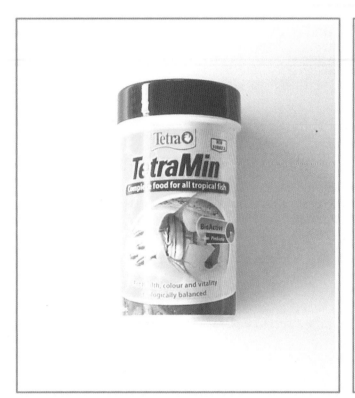

Photographs above showing two of the most well-known flake foods on the market today TetraMin and King British Flake for aquarists – Photographs by Alastair R Agutter

In fact King British was the first food I ever fed to my tropical fish back in 1967, and so as you can see these firms have been around a good while.

However, over the decades from their commercial clout, the Tetra Group have lead the way as a market leader in fish food, and from personal experience, I still buy the product TetraMin today, as I alternate from time to time my flake foods, but there is a distinct difference with the ingredients from one flake food to another.

My own tropical fish seem to prefer King British. Why I cannot say, but they always seem to be far eager to eat this flake food, compared to others like Aquarian that I have tried and used on numerous occasions, to try and mix things up regarding a varied diet.

With regards to feeding my community aquarium fish, I tend to feed them two to three times a day, especially when the fish are at a juvenile stage of growth. When the fish are younger, I tend to feed my tropical fish around 4 to 5 times a day, to help build them up, grow faster and continue to have an eager appetite. When feeding at those times, I use small amounts of food. In other words, little and often!

Photographs above showing a more recent addition to flake foods a brand known as Vitalis and to the right a photograph showing King British Flake Food – Photographs by Alastair R Agutter

The normal rule of thumb and practice over the years and decades, has been to feed just enough food that will be consumed by your tropical fish within a 5 minute period. This is especially pertinent regarding smaller aquarium sizes, for the reason being with smaller Litre or Gallon capacity fish tanks, the water can spoil much easier than an aquarium of a much larger size with a greater volume of water. Little and often also encourages tropical fish to remain eager at feeding times.

Even if fish are more intelligent, evolved and sensitive like Discus (symphysodon), they should always be very keen to eat. In the next set of pictures below, one of the photographs shows some of my Discus just about reaching adult age and size of around 4 inches in diameter and just 12 months old, eagerly eating my own specially prepared food from my hands.

When fish have the right water conditions and the right high protein food, you will always have healthy thriving fish and ones that are not shy, or timid, if the aquariums have been set up in the right location and at the right height, as recommended in the Chapter of the book covering aquarium locations.

Photograph above the Author's Discus feeding out of his hands and the picture to the right showing a close-up of the specially prepared food he makes – Photographs by Alastair R Agutter

With the right healthy diet, you can get fish growing to maturity just as fast as in the wild, or even quicker. Taking Discus (symphysodon) as an example, they do not normally reach adult age until they are around 18 to 24 months old. But these Discus in the above picture, are reaching adult age and size in nearly half the time.

Another secret as mentioned earlier in the book is being able to connect with your tropical fish, where you then have their trust and this goes a very long way, especially surrounding Cichlids. For members of the cichlid family can live for many years, some Discus today since bred in captivity over 25 years ago, are now reaching up to 12, 14, 16 to 18 years in age.

Fish Health and Hygiene at Feeding Times

Now before any feeding is carried out, always remember to give your hands a very good wash with soap and water and then rinse your hands thoroughly with hot water, to ensure there is no soap residue left over on your hands. Then use a clean towel, or tissue (kitchen roll), to dry your hands.

I want you to try and imagine cooking for your loved ones, a delightful meal and then spraying it with aftershave, perfume, or deodorant and then expecting the food to be enthusiastically eaten.

One of the biggest toxicity problems and even killers to tropical fish is the gradual build-up of alcohol based toxins, such as perfumes and aftershaves in the aquarium water. This can be extended to aerosols (air fresheners).

Food given to your tropical fish without washing your hands also becomes tainted and unpalatable from perfumes and aftershaves, resulting in your fish losing their appetite.

Other serious problems that can also arise from not washing your hands, is the great risk of transmitting a virus to your aquarium via the food. This can very often happen during, or after suffering a cold, or flu bout for example, for fish species can catch viruses and do die from them!

The recent events in South America now spreading across the World by Mosquito, this being the Zika Virus, may not only be lethal to human's, but could also be fatal to many countless thousands of Marine and Animal life forms, where new off-spring could well be born with microcephaly disabilities.

At this time in 2016, the media headlines are only focusing on the disease surrounding human activity and this is currently pre-occupying the efforts of Medical Professionals, Zoologists and Marine Biologists world-wide, surrounding the transmission of Zika by Mosquito species.

In the 1980's many aquarists lost Discus (symphysodon) and other exotic tropical fish species from a long drought period, where there became poor water quality across many reservoirs in Europe, yet water from these reservoirs via treatment works was being delivered to the domestic tap water. Aquarists carrying out water changes to their tropical fish soon found that their fish had contracted a virus known as "respiratory distress syndrome," a horrible disease eventually affecting all tropical fish hobbyists aquariums in their homes or fish houses, as the said particular virus once present in water, was able to become airborne and could therefore be transmitted via atmosphere and especially condensation.

So washing your hands on a regular basis is always very important when wanting to keep healthy thriving tropical fish. Thank You!

Flake Fish Food Feeding Times

As you begin your journey of tropical fish keeping, as an Aquarist, it would be prudent and safe to feed your fish twice a day for starters. This should be easy enough to do, regarding work or school commitments by feeding once in the morning before work or school, and then feeding once in the evening upon returning home from work or school.

The normal rule of thumb again is to feed one or two pinches of flake food every feeding time, if you have say between 10 to 30 tropical fish in a naturally planted community aquarium.

Flake foods are obviously mass produced today, with stringent specially prepared recipes by the producers, which include specific ingredients for healthy thriving tropical fish.

The ingredients in flake foods are varied and mixed, with essential ingredients that all fish need in their diet. However, in a community aquarium at feeding times, it can become noticeable that some of your tropical fish have a preference to some of the flake food and not the other.

The main ingredients used for most tropical fish flake foods are;

Composition: Fish derivatives, Cereal, Vegetable Protein Extracts, Yeast derivatives of Vegetable origin, Molluscs and Crustacean, Algae (including Ergosan 2% average, Spirulina 1.7% average), Oils, Fats and Minerals.

Additives Vitamins: Vitamin A 20,000 IU/kg, Vitamin D3 1950 IU/kg, Vitamin E 130IU/kg, Vitamin C (as Li-Ascorbic Acid Monophosphate 676 mg/kg.

Trace Elements: Copper Sulphate Pentahydrate 16mg/kg, Magnesium Oxide 47.21 mg/kg, Zinc Oxide 109.63 mg/kg, Calcium-locate Anhydrous 10.71 mg/kg.

Analytical Constituents: Protein 47%, Fat Content 10%, Crude Fibres 1.5%, Crude Ash 5.5% and ManA 16576 the latter for medical purposes.

The above is a typical ingredient make up of flake foods. However, some flake food recipes will of course vary slightly subject to legal rights and the intellectual property protection of the commercial brand in question.

How Much Flake Food Do Fish Eat

Flake foods can obviously vary in price subject to the amount you purchase. If for example you feed your tropical fish twice a day with flake food and for say 20 to 30 community aquarium fish, they will consume on average between 12 to 18 grams per week. If you are a monthly shopper, this is worth bearing in mind, and so it may be a wise decision to purchase at least a 100 gram container of flake food when you next go shopping, to your local tropical fish shop, or online store. For a flake food amount of this size will last you at least a couple of months hopefully, unless you get some new arrivals in the form of off-spring.

Today also, there is a more varied and wider range of flake foods. One I particularly used years ago, to add to certain specially prepared frozen food was "Tetra Ruby" as this food contains various additional ingredients to help enhance a fish species colours. One of the main ingredients used to help fish develop more colour is "beetroot" and sometimes this root vegetable will be found on the back of some flake food containers, where the ingredients information is provided.

Even larger species of fish still love flake foods and always eager to eat the food, species such as; Angel Fish, Blue Acara, Jack Dempsey, Convict, Ramirez, Kribensis and Firemouth Cichlids to mention a few.

In fact most fish species eat flake food, even Discus when smuggled into frozen recipes of beef heart and liver, or when the fish are particularly young and familiar with the food since birth (fry stage).

How I get fry to eat flake food is to use a spare empty flake food container and get some flake food in my hands and crush it up using my fingers, so the flake food almost goes into a powder form and keep this in the spare container. I normally start to get fry onto flake food after I have been feeding fry with live brine shrimp for several days. However, regarding live bearer species fry, you can start using this method of powdered flake food straight away, as the fry are large enough to consume the crushed flake food.

Live Fish Tropical Foods

Live foods over the years have been a very popular part of the tropical fish diet. Popular live foods being Tubifex, Bloodworms and Daphnia (water fleas).

However, personally speaking I do not feed live foods to any of my fish any longer for a number of very good and sound sensible reasons. The only exception to the rule is the use of brine shrimp. With regards to this exception concerning Brine Shrimp I hatch these, rear and grow these myself in saltwater and are therefore disease free!

Now this cannot be said for other live foods and so please allow me to explain why? But also accompanied with this explanation a little history and background (facts) surrounding tropical fish and live foods, that I believe to be important regarding this case in hand.

In early days of the tropical fish keeping hobby and pastime, Tubifex and Daphnia, were especially popular live foods to feed fish, bloodworms less so, but this was down more to availability of the food.

The reason being in early days for Aquarists to feed live foods was more down to getting tropical fish to eat again. Many cichlids and tropical fish species in the 1950's, 1960's and 1970's especially, were mainly wild caught fish species for the tropical fish hobbyist.

The journeys and transportation of these fish were horrific to say the very least, as some species took several days and weeks to get to certain ports to then be able to fly fish out across the world. Many wild caught species were caught and kept in large metal 50 gallon drums when transported and the water quality was constantly deteriorating all the time both in PH, DH and temperature. Only for the water to be topped up or changed through various stages of this process and so when this livestock finally arrived in the tropical fish retailer's establishment, the poor things were already in a very poor and unhealthy state. The easiest way to get fish back to some form of health was to feed them live foods and then after several weeks with the acclimatization to the new environment the fish if not already sold will start to look slightly better in appearance and hopefully a little healthier before they embark on their next journey to the aquarists home and aquarium.

Now fortunately today, thanks to many dedicated Aquarists and Commercial Breeders around the world and the speed of air freight, most tropical fish today are tank bred and familiar with their surroundings of an aquarium, for most or all are born in them and therefore know no different.

So you can see the logic behind feeding live food to fish that are simply not eating, but there is another way to encourage fish to eat and I will cover this later in the chapter.

Live foods sadly, carry many diseases from their breeding environments and so by feeding your tropical fish live foods you are increasing the risk of disease greatly.

Tubifex

For example is often found in waste pipes or drain sewage works and I am sure you will agree not a very pleasant environment, and the water is full of disease that the Tubifex are transported in. This worm species is very resilient and when feeding to large tropical fish species that may not necessarily be breaking up these worms as they chew. Sometimes these worms will eat and puncture the stomach, or intestine of the fish that has consumed the worms. Another disease known by the feeding of Tubifex is called "Hole in the head" disease and when a fish contracts such an infection, there is very often a fatal outcome for the fish.

Water Daphnia

Often hatches in ponds and pools, where many species of Bird Life visit, to drink, or wash. This Wild Life can carry tapeworms and many other unpleasant intestinal predator diseases including; flukes, nematodes and worms, all of which can be transported through the water, or on the Daphnia to the Aquarists aquarium.

Bloodworms

Are the least lethal of the three live foods mentioned, but the live food still comes from pools and ponds. Bloodworms spend most of their lives in the substrate (mud) of such venues that again house and carry many diseases from existing fish in these pools, or visiting birds and animal wild life.

In Aquarist literature over the years, there can be found many articles regarding these live foods and how to clean them? However, this is an impossible task and the idea of keeping the new live foods in fresh tap water and rinsing through the live foods is <u>NOT</u> full proof!

For one thing most folk are learning today, is that most viruses and diseases have cycles, take "Ebola" for example; after thirty days the virus eggs can hatch again and populate after being dormant in the contracted victims body and in this instance, the victims being in this case the tubifex, bloodworms or daphnia, that are then consumed by your highly loved tropical fish.

Lastly, another reason why I do not use live foods with the exception of microscopic Brine Shrimp for newly hatch fry is when breeding any species of fish including cichlids.

The regular eating of live foods by your fish can and does encourage parents of newly hatched fry to very often go rogue, eating their own young as a result of the frequency of eating live foods. When you have live fry wriggling in a larval state, or free swimming it can be too tempting, resulting in the parents eating the fry.

Frozen Fish Foods

Today the range of frozen foods has greatly widened for tropical fish and I am very pleased to see also the emergence of more specialist high protein frozen foods for Discus and other Cichlid species, these just being two examples.

Photograph above showing pre-packed frozen bloodworms available today from most tropical fish retail outlets and a picture of bloodworm in a bowl – Photographs by Alastair R Agutter

Popular off-the shelf frozen foods today are; Bloodworms, Krill, Daphnia and Lobster Eggs to mention a few.

These off the shelf frozen foods are reasonably priced these days and contribute greatly towards the health of your fish that I describe as "mind, body and soul" from having a healthy varied diet.

Bloodworms in frozen form are a particular favourite with most if not all tropical fish and a worthwhile purchase to include in your freezer.

More specialized frozen foods I like to think derived from Jack Wattley, me and others back in the early to middle of the 1980's when trying to develop high protein foods for Discus fish especially. From such humble endeavours, in those earlier years, a whole new industry exists today, where commercial breeders and tropical fish product producers and manufacturers offer a whole host of these foods for cichlids, catfish and other species.

So what is a high protein fish food and what can it do?

Well, high protein specially prepared foods is like the difference in performance between a family saloon car compared to a formula one racing car.

High protein foods are just irresistible to the fish and so healthy where you can literally see your fish growing week on week. Taking Discus that are very close to my heart after breeding them in captivity, with high protein specially prepared foods, I can get these species from fry stage to adulthood in just twelve months, as opposed to the normal growth and age to adult hood being around 24 months. Also with high protein foods the fish become very healthy and their body mass is noticeable. For with regards to Discus fed on high protein food, they are a lot larger and more heavily set in the body.

At the beginning of this chapter is a photograph of one of my high protein foods that I feed to my fish and will take you through the recipe now and accompanied with photographs. As I have promised to many folk in and out of the industry, that I would provide a new recipe of a high protein food that is irresistible to Discus, Angel Fish, Catfish and many other Cichlids and also tropical fish community members including Neon's, Cardinals, Guppies, Platies, Tetras and barbs etc.

High protein foods are specially prepared so they have all the main and essential minerals and vitamins that tropical fish require in their diet. By providing high protein food it ensures your tropical fish are at their most healthiest and therefore far more resilient in the event of contracting a disease, or seeking to bring your tropical fish into a breeding condition.

This particular recipe when fed to my Angel Fish for example will bring the pairs into breeding condition within two weeks and where they will spawn and continue to do so every fortnight, for a number weeks and months in 10 to 14 day cycles.

Beef Heart and Spinach High Protein Super Fish Food

When making this recipe and others, some essential tools will be required and these are; Scissors, Small Spoon, Small Glass, Wooden Spoon, Sharp Knife (small), Large Bowl (plastic, or stainless steel), Small Clear Freezer Bags and an Electronic Blender or Mixer.

This recipe will make up around 20 packs of frozen high protein food for your tropical fish and can be grated from frozen and fed once a day as part of their diet.

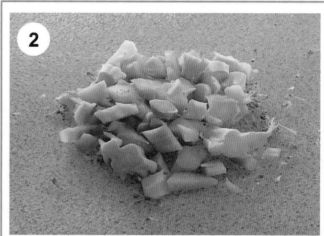

Photographs above showing 1/. Broccoli Tops 2/. Broccoli Stems 3/. Blender Dicing Broccoli 4/. Broccoli Diced in Mixing Bowl – Photographs by Alastair R Agutter

1/. Take 1 pound of Broccoli and cut into manageable pieces using a small sharp knife and then place in the Electric Blender or Mixer, then switch on for about 5 to 6 seconds or until the Broccoli is diced into very small pieces (not liquidized). See pictures 1, 2, 3 and 4 above.

2/. Take 1 pound of Spinach and wash thoroughly in a colander under cold water and then cut the spinach into small manageable pieces, using a small sharp knife. Then place small batches of the spinach into the Electric Blender or Mixer and dice into small pieces as you did before with the Broccoli. Please see picture 5 below.

Photographs above showing 5/. Spinach and Broccoli Diced in the Mixing Bowl 6/. Lamb or Beef Liver 7/. Lamb or Beef Liver Cut into small pieces 8/. Diced Beef or Lamb Liver added to the Mixing Bowl – Photographs by Alastair R Agutter

3/. Take 1 pound of Beef or Lamb Liver and cut into small pieces using a small sharp knife and remove any fat or gristle tissue from the liver. Then take small batches of the Beef or Lamb Liver and place in the Electric Blender or Mixer to dice the Liver.

Then finally place the diced Beef or Lamb Liver into mixing bowl already containing the Broccoli and Spinach. Please see pictures 6, 7 and 8 above.

3/. Take 1 pound of Beef or Lamb Liver and cut into small pieces using a small sharp knife and remove any fat or gristle tissue from the liver.

Then take small batches of the Beef or Lamb Liver and place in the Electric Blender or Mixer to dice the Liver.

Then finally place the diced Beef or Lamb Liver into mixing bowl already containing the Broccoli and Spinach. Please see pictures 6, 7 and 8 above.

Next take the Beef Heart and start cutting into small pieces using a small sharp knife, removing all fat and gristle from the meat.

Then place the pieces of Beef Heart into the Electric Blender or Mixer for a few seconds each time or until the Beef Heart is diced and then place the diced Beef Heart into the mixing bowl with the other ingredients. Please see pictures 11 and 12.

Above showing 9/. Beef Heart 10/. Broccoli, Spinach, Beef Heart and Liver 11/. Cut Beef Heart 12/. Diced Broccoli, Spinach, Liver, Beef Heart and Peeled Prawns – Photographs by Alastair R Agutter

Next take half a pound of fresh North Atlantic Cold Peeled Prawns (not frozen) and place these in the Electric Blender, or Mixer, to dice the prawns. Then place the peeled diced prawns into the mixing bowl along with the other ingredients.

Photographs above showing 17/. Multi Vitamins dissolved in a small amount of water 18/. Sachets of Gelatine, Spoon and Small Sharp Knife – Photographs by Alastair R Agutter

Next take two Multi Vitamin Tablets (200 mg) and place these in a small glass. Then pour a small amount of water into the glass over the Multi Vitamin Tablets and stir with a small spoon, until the Multi Vitamin tablets are completely dissolved. Once the Multi Vitamins are completely dissolved in the glass, pour the contents of the glass into the mixing bowl with the other ingredients. Please see picture 17 above.

Next take a sachet of Gelatine or Gluten as it is known in the USA and empty the sachet contents into a small glass (tumbler, whiskey glass size). Then boil a kettle of water and pour a small amount of the boiling water over the Gelatine (gluten) in the glass, to around half full. Give the glass with the gelatine and water a good stir with a spoon.

Photographs above showing 13/. Mixed ingredients Recipe in Bowl 14/. Putting Mixed Recipe into small clear freezer bags 15/. Mixed Recipe patted down into small flat blocks in clear freezer bags 16/. Flat Freezer Bag Fish Food placed in a tray – Photographs by Alastair R Agutter

Once the Gelatine sachet contents are completely dissolved in the glass, pour the contents of the glass with the gelatine into the other mixing bowl holding all other ingredients. Please see picture 18 showing Gelatine (gluten).

Next, take a wooden spoon and then thoroughly mix the contents of the bowl by hand stirring continually all the ingredients in the mixing bowl until the mix is evenly distributed.

Once the contents are mixed thoroughly, get some small clear freezer bags around 6 x 8 inches and start putting some of the fish food into the bags, using a wooden spoon. Then pat down the fish food in the freezer bags making them into thin small slabs about 6 inches long and about 4 inches wide and about ½ to 3/8 of an inch thick, about 8 to 12 mm in new money as they say. Make sure you fold the ends of the freezer bags under the fish food slabs so the fish food in the bags are sealed and closed. Next get a plastic tray or small container and place the packs of fish food on the tray, or in the plastic tray container. The containers I use are from previous purchases of meat in trays from supermarkets. I wash these trays out thoroughly and use them for this process of freezing my fish food, as they are ideal for the job and you can place around 4 to 5 thin packs (slabs) of your fish food in each tray. Please see pictures 13, 14, 15 and 16 above.

Once all the fish food has been placed in the freezer bags, patted down into slabs and placed in or on trays. Simply pop the trays of fish food into your freezer.

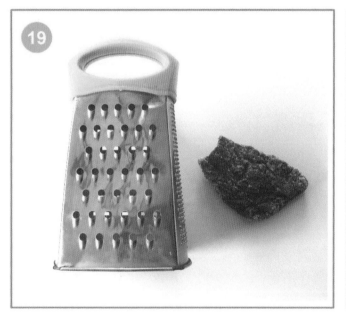 

Photographs above showing 19/. Grater and a piece of fish food frozen slab to grate 20/. Grated fish food from the slab in a bowl ready to feed to your fish – Photographs by Alastair R Agutter

Once your fish food has been frozen, it is now ready to use. Simply take a slab of fish food out of the freezer and gently peel back the freezer bag away from the frozen food. Then take a normal cheese grater and use the course setting in the picture above and grate downwards your frozen fish food onto a plate, or into a bowl. Please see picture 19 and 20 above.

Your fish food is then ready to give to your fish. At first feed sparingly for the first day or so, then after that period feed as much fish food the fish can eat within a five minute period. Once your tropical fish become use to this new food, they will eat it as if the food is going out of fashion.

This fish food is so successful with my fish they even turn their noses up to the bloodworm, if I try to feed the bloodworm to my fish at the same time, when feeding this beef heart recipe. My tropical fish simply prefer this specially prepared high protein food above all else, especially cichlids and catfish.

Beef Heart Broccoli and Spinach Recipe

Ingredients:

1 pound of Broccoli

1 pound of Spinach

3 pound of Beef Heart

1 pound of Beef or Lamb Liver

½ pound of Peeled Prawns

2 Multi Vitamin Tablets (200 mg)

1 Sachet of Gelatine (gluten)

The above recipe is suitable for juvenile and adult fish. The following recipe is for smaller fish and the process of making and preparing the fish food is exactly the same as explained before.

Beef Heart Broccoli and Spinach Junior Recipe

The following recipe is for smaller fish including very young cichlid fish species.

Ingredients:

1 pound of Broccoli

1 pound of Spinach

3 pound of Beef Heart

1 pound of Beef or Lamb Liver

½ pound of Herring or Cod Roe

1 Multi Vitamin Tablets (100 mg)

1 Vitamin D Tablet (80mg)

In this recipe **NO** Gelatine (gluten) is used to bind the fish food.

Beef Heart and Spinach Ruby Recipe

Ingredients:

1 pound of Broccoli

1 pound of Spinach

3 pound of Beef Heart

1 pound of Beef or Lamb Liver

½ pound of Peeled Prawns

2 cooked beetroots (peeled + chopped + diced)

2 Multi Vitamin Tablets (200 mg)

1 Vitamin D Tablet (80mg)

1 Sachet of Gelatine (gluten)

The above recipe is suitable for juvenile and adult fish with additional ingredients for bone development and colour enhancement radiance.

Pellet Freeze Dried Fish Foods

Another range and type of tropical fish foods available on the market for today's Aquarists are pellets and freeze dried foods.

Photographs above showing Freeze Dried Daphnia in Packet Form and also the Freeze Dried Daphnia poured into a bowl for recognition purposes – Photographs by Alastair R Agutter

With regards to freeze dried foods I should say they are great for your fish, but that's not me. I love all fish and all animals and only want the best for them. So freeze dried foods cannot beat the real thing with regards to fresh frozen foods.

Freeze dried foods maybe handy in the event of an emergency from running out of fish food and where there is nothing else available.

Freeze dried food is very fibrous and I should imagine, it's like eating lumps of shredded wheat without any milk or sugar!

There is undoubtedly a wide and varied range of freeze dried foods today on the market and to encourage the eating of such a food by your tropical fish, must be based on scent and smell of the fish food in question.

This then leads us into the realms of artificial additives, and where I have never been a fan of such engineered chemicals for the food industry, be it human, pet or animal.

Many ailments and illnesses today, including very serious life threatening health problems in the form of Cancers, Alzheimer's, Multiple Cerosis, Liver, Kidney and Heart disease are caused from NOT eating healthy wholesome natural foods. Such processed foods for human, or animal consumption, I find to be very serious, commercially negligent and deeply worrying.

Pellets foods for tropical and cold water fish have now been around for several decades and offering today a wide and varied range.

The food is easy to administer and hassle free for aquarists and comes in many varying sizes and formula recipes for different types of fish species.

Two main forms are floating and sinking pellets. With regards to floating pellets, they can drift around on the surface of the aquarium for quite a while and can cause a protein build up around the surface walls of the aquarium if not eaten almost immediately. However, these pellets are very hard from the processing procedure and do expand in water and this could cause bloat to fish if they consume too many pellets that expand in the stomach.

Photographs above showing Freeze Dried Daphnia in Packet Form and also the Freeze Dried Daphnia poured into a bowl for recognition purposes – Photographs by Alastair R Agutter

Most pellets are cereal based, but they do include additives in the recipe and can cause constipation to fish if they are not being fed a balanced diet.

Sinking pellets can cause fish to root around on the bottom of the aquarium and this can be destructive to established plant life (root systems). Fish can also dig up and disturb trapped biological cultures breaking down waste material and also disturb pockets of toxins and chemicals being naturally broken down in the aquarium.

Whereas with flake and fresh frozen food, when the fish food does drop through the water it is invariably eaten before reaching the bottom (substrate) of the aquarium.

Flake and fresh frozen food is much lighter and if it does drop to the bottom of the aquarium it normally just lightly sits or suspends itself just above the substrate, where fish can very quickly and easily swim along gathering up eating the food and as a result, causing no harm to the substrate or plant life environment in the aquarium.

Finally, pellet foods can cause aquariums to become cloudy if overfed by a lazy aquarist and also resulting in a bacterial build-up in the aquarium, including the populating of infusoria and micro worms.

Recent years and today, the jury is still out on pellet foods for farmed fish!

Aquarists Fish Care

I wanted to write this feature as a supportive part of your new or existing pastime of tropical fish keeping. This section is especially pertinent and relevant to the establishing of a new aquarium and the 28 to 30 day rule.

Photograph above showing one of the Author's Naturally Planted Aquarium's in Early Days with the inclusion of a gradual build-up of fish inhabitants – Photograph by Alastair R Agutter

The first thing to remember when keeping fellow creatures is the great burden of responsibility that falls upon our shoulders to love and care, to do the very best for our new family members.

There will be challenging moments as is the case in all walks of life and in our noble pastime of tropical fish keeping.

These moments will include sadly, the occasional loss of an inhabitant member from an illness. This can often happen more so at the beginning of an Aquarist's journey and these moments should not serve to discourage folk from keeping tropical fish, for these events happen to most if not all Aquarists at the very start.

One of the biggest processes and moments in tropical fish keeping is the establishing of an aquarium and creating a biological bacterial environment. Now a great deal of confusion is created surrounding this subject even today, and in truth there is no silver bullet, or method to bye-pass the natural process of creating a biological environment.

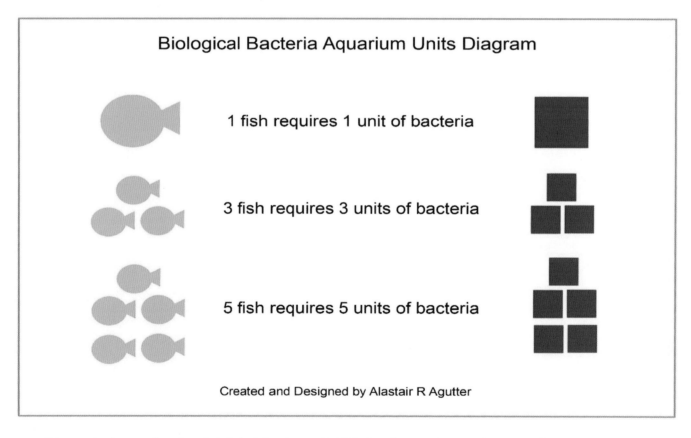

Diagram above showing fish inhabitants and biological bacterial culture in unit form to help show interdependency of both element parties – Diagram by Alastair R Agutter

No chemicals or products on the market will give you instant results or perfect water conditions for tropical fish. Even with our technology today, we still have to give reverence and respect Mother Nature and where only she can create, begin and establish an inhabitable biological eco-system for marine and plant life.

Pictured above, I have created a simple diagram surrounding the biological process, for even whilst writing this book, I have read folks requests for advice and help surrounding setting up breeding and rearing tanks as a result of their tropical fish spawning, where they need to establish a new aquarium and still struggle to rationalize the process of a biological culture. This is even when very experienced commercial industry players on forums online have tried to articulate the process.

The best way to look at the process of establishing an aquarium is to look at the fish and the biological process in units. Now when you do not have an established biological culture, any fish you enter into an aquarium requires a biological culture to breakdown fish waste matter. So if we add one fish to a new aquarium, we need one unit of bacterial culture to process the fish waste and by-products. One unit of a bacterial culture created, has less impact in an aquarium, than if you were to introduce ten fish in an aquarium and where as a result, you will require ten units of a biological bacterial culture to be established.

With the presence of plants when establishing a new aquarium, they can greatly help in the process of establishing safe aquarium water conditions by filtering out toxins and waste, for plants actually have their own bacterial culture already in existence on the plants themselves.

So as for a bacterial culture being established in a filter medium for example, the plants are already doing some of the heavy lifting for the aquarist, as the aquarium becomes a naturally safe environment as we cycle through ammonia, nitrites to nitrate.

So the least pressure on any new aquarium environment the better, while this biological bacterial process is being established. So this is why in the 28 to 30 day rule when establishing an aquarium, I urge new aquarists to only buy initially a very small number of tropical fish in the 1's and 2's and to gradually build up in fish numbers overtime.

The reality is, to have a biological bacterial process in an aquarium you need a fish for the bacteria to grow and exist, to feed from the fish waste by-products. If you have the bacteria and no fish, the bacteria will die!

Feeding fish in such a new environment needs to be in small amounts and measured, ensuring no food is left, as this will help keep a control on the biological bacterial culture development and thus in turn, keeping ammonia and nitrite levels down during this process, before nitrate begins to grow and populate to counter and digest the nitrite oxides.

Carryout regular water changes as directed, this will remove and help keep down the build-up of any ammonia or nitrites.

Check fish for health issues by making sure your fish species eyes are clear, for cloudy eyes is a sign of ammonia and nitrite bacterial build-up in the aquarium water.

Keep an eye on fish inhabitant behaviour patterns, if your fish start to swim and rub against objects in the aquarium, this again is a sign of bacterial build-up in the form of ammonia and nitrite. Again this just requires regular water changes, NO chemicals.

If fish show signs of white spot or damage to the fins, this again is a sign of bacterial build up or the aquarium water temperature being too low. Check your heater thermostat by waiting to see if the neon light is coming on and working properly, indicating that your heater thermostat is functioning.

Check your thermometer to see what temperature the aquarium water is and increase the heater thermostat accordingly, if the temperature is too low. Regular water changes and the increase of water temperature will cure any fin rot or white spot.

As like all humans, when we are run down and low as a result of stress, diet or the environment, we come out in spots and this is the case with tropical fish.

Again no chemicals are required to cure an ailment such as white spot, or fin rot. All chemicals in such a situation if used, just further complicates the situation even more by increasing the contamination in the water, hence the need for regular water changes only.

Tropical Fish Species

In every issue of the "Tropical Fish Keeping Journal" more tropical fish species will be featured and referenced for aquarists.

Picture 1/. Kribensis (Pelvicachromis taeniatus) – Picture 2/. Angel Fish (Pterophylium Scalare)

Name: Kribensis Cichlid

Species Name: *Pelvicachromis taeniatus*

Summary Description: Kribensis are dwarf cichlids and native to the regions of Cameroon and Nigeria in Africa. Kribensis inhabit mostly soft-water rivers throughout the above regions and can be a brightly coloured fish species, especially at breeding times displaying a cherry red belly colouration more predominantly on the female member of the species.

Kribensis in an aquarium environment are most suited to being with their own and very often Aquarists tend to put species such as Tiger Barbs with them.

Member Family Genera: Cichlidae

Region(s): Cameroon and Nigeria in Africa

Disposition: Shows Aggressive Behaviour Patterns

Average Adult Size: 2.5 to 3 inches

Average Temperature: 76 to 82 Fahrenheit

PH Range: 6.0 to 7.6 PH

Diet: Small Cichlid Pellets and Flake Foods

Reproduction: Egg Layers

Lifespan: 4 to 5 years

Name: Angel Fish

Species Name: *Pterophylium Scalare*

Summary Description: Angel fish are one of the more unusual looking tropical fish cichlid species who are native to South America, primarily the Great River Amazon.

They can be compatible in community aquariums, as long as they are in small numbers of only one or two. When in large numbers establishing a pecking order to pair off and breed, the fish can be extremely aggressive towards each other and species in the aquarium.

Member Family Genera: Cichlidae

Region(s): South America

Disposition: Compatible for Community Aquariums

Average Adult Size: 10 to 12 inches high including fins, 4 to 6 inches long

Average Temperature: 78 to 84 Fahrenheit

PH Range: 6.0 to 7.8 PH

Diet: Small Cichlid Pellets, Vegetation, Beef Heart and Flake Foods

Reproduction: Egg Layers

Lifespan: 5 to 10 years

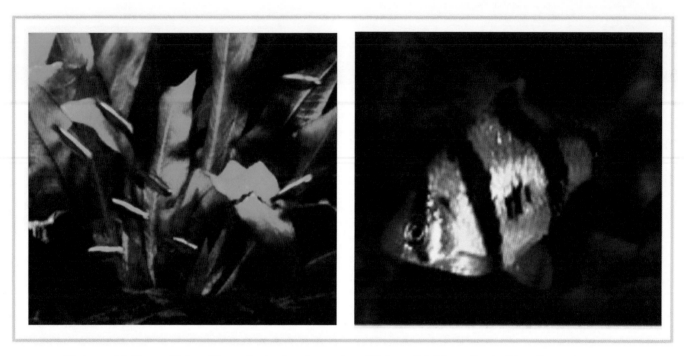

Picture 1/. Neon Tetra (Paracheirodon innesi) – Picture 2/. Tiger Barb (Puntius tetrazona)

Name: Neon Tetra

Species Name: *Paracheirodon innesi*

Summary Description: The Neon Tetra is one of the stars in the tropical fish keeping world and renowned for their translucent iridescent colours. I think when folk relate to tropical fish keeping, the Neon Tetra is the species that provides those lasting images and memories of our noble pastime. There is nothing more stunning than seeing a shoal of Neon Tetra's travelling past a sunken piece of bogwood in a magical underwater world in one's home. Neon Tetras are easy to keep in a community aquarium, but are known for being a difficult species to breed in captivity. However, the Dutch have now got the method of breeding these species in captivity down to a fine art.

Member Family Genera: Characidae

Region(s): Columbia, Peru and Brazil in South America

Disposition: Excellent Community Aquarium Fish

Average Adult Size: 1.2 to 1.5 inches

Average Temperature: 68 to 84 Fahrenheit

PH Range: 5.5 to 7.8 PH

Diet: Varied Diet, Vegetation and Flake Foods

Reproduction: Egg Scatterers

Lifespan: 2 to 3 years

Tiger Barb

Species Name: *Puntius tetrazona*

Summary Description: Tigers Barbs I think are another one of those fish species in tropical fish keeping that folk remember and relate too regarding the hobby. Tiger Barbs have a bright golden body with black vertical stripes and the fins of the species are of a bright red colouration. When in shoals, Tiger Barbs do look stunning in an aquarium. Tiger Barbs can be aggressive and very much a nipping fish towards others and so I would air caution when considering these for a community aquarium. Very often shoals of Tiger Barbs can be found in Aquarists aquariums who are also keeping smaller members of the cichlid family such as Kribensis, Blue Acara and Ramirez Dwarf Cichlids.

Member Family Genera: Cyprinidae

Region(s): Central and Eastern Asia

Disposition: Can be Aggressive, Nipping

Average Adult Size: 2 to 2.75 inches

Average Temperature: 76 to 82 Fahrenheit

PH Range: 6.0 to 8.0 PH

Diet: Varied Diet, Flake Foods

Reproduction: Egg Layers

Lifespan: 2 to 3 years

Aquatic Plant Species

In this issue of the Tropical Fish Keeping Journal Edition Book Four, is another featured a selection of aquatic plant species accompanied with fact files.

Aquatic Plant Fact File:

Name of Specie: *Cabomba Caroliniana*

Summary Description: *Cabomba has been a very popular aquatic plant for countless generations in ponds, tropical fish and cold water aquariums. Very easy to maintain and very adaptable for varying water quality and thrives in bright light conditions. The plant is ideal to be used as a background display.*

Propagation: *Cuttings from the Plant*

Average Height: *18 – 22 inches*

Native Region: *Central and South America*

Temperatures: *70 to 82 degrees Fahrenheit*

Aquatic Plant Fact File:

Name of Specie: *Elodea Canadensis*

Summary *Description: Elodea is commonly known as Canadian pond weed and very often found to be a floating plant. Most Elodea plants acquired are female when found in Western Europe and Eurasia and very rarely flowers as a perennial. Elodea can be planted in a pot or substrate in bunches of five or six strands for best effect, but very often fairs better as a floating plant. The plant is ideal to be used as a background display.*

Propagation: *Cuttings from the Plant*

Average Height: *18 to 22 inches*

Native Region: *North America, Europe*

Temperatures: *48 – 68 degrees Fahrenheit*

Aquarium Maintenance and Care Guide

1/. Firstly, always remember to switch off heater thermostat as part of the maintenance process and give the heater thermostat a good clean and wipe, then switch back on the device.

Aquarium maintenance on a regular monthly basis can be an invaluable habit to adopt to ensure all your hard work is not in vain from technical failure – Photograph by Alastair R Agutter

2/. Carry out a quick check around the aquarium to make sure there are no leaks and that the Aquarium Stand is still safe and secure.

3/. Check the lighting system to make sure no part of the electrical light element system is being exposed to water, condensation or dampness.

4/. Check all plugs and electrical connections to make sure they are still safe and secure and only 3 Amp fuses used.

5/. Check the filter system to make sure there are no loose fittings in the way of pipes or airline connectors if using canister, air pump, sump or reservoir filtration systems.

6/. Check all of the Aquarium's glass and then using a small clean sponge or several pieces of kitchen roll crunched up and wipe the front glass of the aquarium internally to remove any algae build-up.

7/. Check to make sure any condensation trays are clean and free of any algae build-up and functioning properly by covering the aquarium water surface area efficiently.

Fish Species Safety and Health Care

In the next chapter we cover fish diseases that can occur and where the aquarist needs some answers. This chapter is more devoted to preventative cure, so your tropical fish do not become ill.

Health and Fish Care

Happy healthy tropical fish means disease free members of the family household and for your love and care they will connect with you – Photograph by Alastair R Agutter

1/. The first golden rule with regards to tropical fish and aquariums is to never tap on the glass. It's like the equivalent to someone coming up behind you and blasting you with a claxon directly in your ear. Tapping on the glass causes electromagnetic shock waves and the amplification of sound through the water that can cause permanent damage.

2/. Aquarium location is critical, make sure the aquarium is placed in the correct position so your tropical fish members of your family can see the coming and going of the family and visitors.

There is nothing worse than someone creeping up on you and making you jump. This is the same for your tropical fish and stress is one of the biggest killers of tropical fish.

3/. Regular feeding and a varied diet with good quality high protein foods including flake food for most community species will see healthy thriving fish and growing to their full potential. Feeding needs to be carried out at regular times if once, twice, three or four times a day. Feeding your fish at the same time prevents fighting and the hoarding of food by other more dominant species in the aquarium that can contribute to the contamination of the water. Fish do know these times from their very own body clock mechanism and sunlight activity in a home or fish house.

4/. Regular water changes are another key preventative to ensuring healthy thriving tropical fish. Most diseases come about from fish becoming stressed as a result of a lack of routine, poor water quality leading to disease.

5/. The right food is also critical as mentioned above, no one would want to eat egg and chips every day for the rest of their lives and so fish do need a regular and varied diet, so the fish continue to be eager to eat.

6/. Correct temperatures are obviously critical regarding the health of tropical fish, so always make sure from the outset that you have the correct heater thermostat to meet the aquariums requirements for successfully heating the aquarium water in the fish tank. A table to help establish the correct heating requirements can be found in the heating chapter of the book and also the chapter containing reference tables.

7/. Correct filtration rates are very important to ensure the filtration system is biologically processing waste at a rate where the passing of the waste matter can be broken down successfully, resulting in clean quality water on exit of the filter system.

8/. Correct Lighting is essential for both plants and tropical fish to thrive. For plants, light is required to help them grow and eat by carrying out the photosynthesis process and with regards to tropical fish, for their growth and bone development. Again also having a lighting system that is scheduled that comes on at specific times and go off at set times is most desired.

Fish Diseases and Cures

Sometimes when acquiring new fish for your aquarium, some species maybe infected with some common disorders such as gill flukes, worms and white spot etc. But all can be cured with tender love and care.

The Fish Whisperer – A Complete bond and trust between Author and Discus Fish, as the Juvenile comes up to feed from Alastair's fingers – Photograph by Alastair R Agutter

When fish are diseased for the new tropical fish keeper, this can be a very stressful period for fear of losing fish, but in such scenarios it does not have to be an alarming or worrying time. On such occasions it just requires the Aquarist to carry out a few activities to get things right!

For your peace of mind such events I have experienced throughout my fish keeping life first hand and now spanning some 5 decades (50 years) this coming year in 2017. So please do not worry, as I will provide you here in this chapter the best course of action if such an event should arise.

Most fish diseases come about as a result of stress, or water quality, and if we relate this to our own lives with regards to living in a densely polluted environment and unable to coup, it would only be a matter of time before we became ill.

As you know from reading the book so far, I try to avoid any form of chemicals, as they can cause long term lasting effects, especially when it comes to wanting species to breed in captivity and growth I might add.

Some treatments can cause more stress to fish, rather than serving as a cure, and very often most common diseases can be resolved with just a little effort as mentioned earlier by the aquarist, in relation to improving the water quality, altering the temperature and improving the diet for his or her tropical fish.

As like all our Wild Life that grace this Earth we call home, fish are fascinating creatures. Fish species like all other creatures, live each day, learning and evolving, as set down by the rules of the Divine Covenant in relation to Natural Law.

Even in my 50 years as an Aquarist I am still learning, and this process will continue for an eternity I am sure. But from my study, and one of the most popular topics in Town regarding the Science, Biology and Medical Community today being discussed is consciousness. Recent experiments with our cousins the Dolphins surrounding mirrors has proved these beloved creatures can recognize and acknowledge it is they, who is seen in the mirrors reflection. From communication by such species as just one example and the ability to collaborate, brings with it consciousness "emotion" and coupled to this at times is stress and anxiety that causes illness and disease.

When you have studied tropical fish species for so long and especially the more highly evolved and intelligent species, such as cichlids, and none more so than the Discus, it is possible to connect!

The signs of healthy fish, especially juveniles is when they are eating and then fighting, such activity confirms survival mode has passed, this meaning water conditions and the environment is fine.

Very often most cases where fish species will not eat or show signs of sickness (ill) is stress related, sometimes even losing the will to live. Now to some this may seem farfetched, but in truth as we have to become more aware of our environment from Climate Change, and the very grave impact this will have on us.

For the very first time, regarding the Human Story and Journey, we are now beginning to start scratching beyond the surface of these very important topics and subjects. I hope for the very first time in the Human Story there is a glimmer of light with the realization that our survival is only possible by learning to co-exist with all other life forms. So for us to achieve this feat of greater understanding, we must begin by finally consigning ignorance to the bin! Here below I have set out for you many, if not most of the ailments that tropical fish contract.

Today thankfully, as a result of most fish being tank bred by commercial breeders in captivity, the risk of disease has been greatly reduced in comparison to bringing in tropical fish from the wild. A good varied diet, regular routine and regular water changes will deliver disease free healthy thriving fish, but in the event of disease here follows diseases symptoms and cures.

Diseases Symptoms and Cures

The first thing you need to know is the following cures applied to the diseases covered below, are based on my very own first-hand experience and from my research I have endeavoured to find the safest cures and remedies.

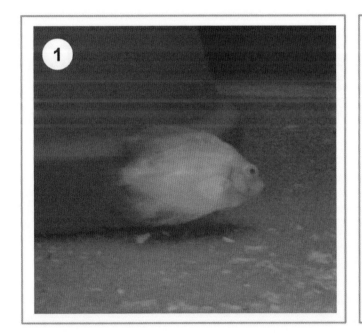 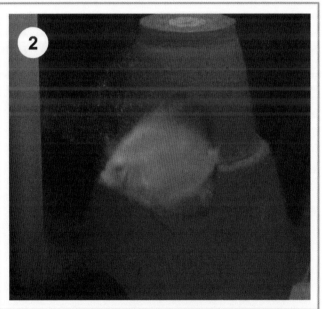

Pic 1/. Shows a Young Discus not eating from stress and Pic 2/. Shows the same Discus just two weeks later eating high protein food and putting on weight – Photographs by Alastair R Agutter

The above pictures show the same Discus, she was a small 1-1/2" fish that I found in a retail outlet with a deformed mouth, she was on her last legs and about to die see picture one. I hate seeing fish suffer like that and so I purchased the small Discus from the shop and brought her home with me. I then placed her in an aquarium with some very small ember tetra's (5) and began feeding her one of my juvenile high protein beef heart recipes that can be found in the book's food chapter and in just 24 hours at the right temperature, the right water conditions and the right food, she began to eat. Some two weeks later she had put weight on, her eyes had cleared see picture two and now she is swimming about with other fellow juvenile Discus species of the same size holding her own and happy!

I know the above photograph is not pleasant where you see a fish suffer.

But I wanted to show you how many diseases are caused by stress and the cure is not from the use of chemicals.

Today, if you are interested in the progress of this little fish. She is now with 7 other Discus friends and very bossy, in fact she is one of the very first to get to the food and will be around 3 inches in diameter in the coming few weeks and very heavily set.

Tropical Fish Disease Guide

Symptoms: Eye Discolouration and Cloudiness

Cause: Bacterial build-up, insufficient water changes

Treatment: Water changes immediately of natural localized tap water and warmed to the aquarium temperature. Replace as much as about 50% of the water and carry this out every other day for a week (3 to 4 times).

Symptoms: Skin reaction, patches.

Cause: The fish is fielding a barrier, Bacterial infection by Costia or Protozoan.

Treatment: Again regular water changes of localized tap water and the chlorinated content should kill the bacterial disease. 50% water changes again every other day for a week. If no improvement carry out these water changes every day for a further week.

Symptoms: Respiratory Distress Syndrome, Choking

Cause: Gill worm or flukes

Treatment: Introduce an Oxydator into the Aquarium and further air stones. Carry out regular daily water changes of 50% using localized tap water that retains small amounts of chlorine that should kill the creatures infecting the fish. Carry this out until the signs of the erratic behaviour from the fish including hitting objects when swimming or gasping for air.

Symptoms: White transparent faeces, darkening of the fish's colour.

Cause: Spiro nucleus, sometime created unknowingly by stress.

Treatment: Place the affected fish with some smaller fish that have a healthy appetite to encourage feeding again and confidence.

Symptoms: Release of transparent strings from around the head region

Cause: Hole in the head disease caused by infection transmitted by Tubifex worms and some other live foods.

Treatment: Make regular water changes and increase the temperature of the aquarium water by 5 degrees. In many instances the disease has affected the brain and little can be done. Some treatments are extreme and can kill the fish from further stress.

Symptoms: Hunger strikes

Cause: Water conditions poor, intestinal disorders

Treatment: Raise the temperature of the aquarium by 5 degrees, make daily water changes (50%) and introduce live foods such as blood worms or daphnia. The fish should be up and around in no time.

Symptoms: Long white stringy faeces

Cause: Tapeworms or Nematodes

Treatment: 50% water changes using regular tap water every day that your fish are accustomed too. Hopefully the chlorinated water will cure the disease, or drive out the intestinal predators.

Symptoms: Skin disease or skin infections

Cause: Bacterial infection from poor quality water conditions.

Treatment: 50% water changes each day for a week using local accustomed chlorinated tap water. These water changes will remove any bacterial build-up. You can also introduce a sponge filter to further assist in the event that your existing filter is faulty or struggling to deal with these events.

Symptoms: Fish growths on skin or fins

Cause: Bacterial infections

Treatment: 50% water changes each day for a week using local acclimatized chlorinated tap water. These water changes will remove any bacterial build up.

Symptoms: Black body lying on the sides, high shimmying movements

Cause: The Plague

Treatment: Airborne viral infection. Turn all lights off and increase the temperature by 5 degrees, carry out a 50% water changes and introduce some live food like daphnia and leave the fish in peace and quiet as they are highly stressed.

Symptoms: Swelling around the Stomach Region of the Fish and Lighter in Colouration

Cause: Constipation

Treatment: Sometimes fish do suffer from constipation, this is often caused where fish have been purchased from a retail outlet and not been eating properly. Then when the fish is in the new surroundings with the right conditions, the fish can sometimes gorge food and then end up with constipation, as they have not been passing waste properly for some time. In these circumstances you can only hope that the fish will eventually begin the pass the waste build-up, sometimes the fish will jolt or look as if it is doing a dance in the water as it tries to shift the waste matter. Sometimes the fish may hit itself against an object trying to rid itself of the problem. Very often with this condition the fish will stop eating and hopefully the food waste is eventually passed.

Symptoms: Swelling of Stomach

Cause: Bloat

Treatment: Bloat is similar to constipation, but can be long lasting and fatal where fish have eaten in excess for long periods of time and damaged internal organs sometimes from fighting.

There is no cure with this condition only hope that nature will take its course and he fish recovers over time.

_____

Symptoms: Dorsal Tail and Pectoral Fin Damage

Cause: Bullying

Treatment: All fish have a pecking order amongst their own species and other aquarium inhabitants and where fighting breaks out. Some fish deliberately attack dorsal, tail and pectoral fins. This bullying behaviour can commence during and after feeding times, sometimes as a result of not enough food being fed to the fish in the community aquarium. Increase feeding to see if this helps alleviate the bickering and fighting.

_____

Symptoms: White Spots on Body and Fins

Cause: Stress and Anxiety

Treatment: White spot is a very common disease and caused from stress and anxiety, that is brought about by too lower temperatures in most cases and water quality. Simply increase the temperature of the aquarium by around 5 degrees and carryout a 50% water change. After a few days the fish species suffering from this condition should begin to recover. Another common reason for white spot, if we are referring to just one fish in an aquarium, this condition could be down to bullying, so keep a good eye on the fish suffering and see if there is any bullying taking place from other fish.

Symptoms: Fin Deterioration (Fin Rot)

Cause: Stress and Anxiety

Treatment: Fin Rot again is often caused from stress as a result of poor water quality. Carryout a 50% water change and raise the temperature of the aquarium by around 5 degrees. This should reduce the bacterial build-up including the toxins and oxides in the water such as Ammonia, Nitrites and Nitrates. Adding chemicals to the water in any form such as Methylene Blue, only further adds more toxins to the water and creates more stress to the fish inhabitants.

Aquarists Products Guide

Welcome to the **"Aquarists Products Guide"** in the **"Tropical Fish Keeping Journal"** book edition four, featuring more reliable products personally recommended and used. n

Fish Foods: Today in tropical fish keeping, we have far more advanced and developed products available to us and ranging in price to meet every Aquarists budget and needs.

Picture above showing more user-friendly and green product tropical fish foods for today's aquarist with biodegradable containers – Photograph compiled by Alastair R Agutter

A wide and varied diet ensures your tropical fish are receiving essential vitamins, trace elements and proteins in their diet for healthy thriving inhabitants in your aquarium.

Natural fats are also important in a fish species diet to help build-up fish for reproduction.

Reproduction in a fish species life cycle can really take its toll and more so regarding some highly evolved species such as cichlids, where so often after hatching cichlids will look after their young (fry) and fail to eat themselves through these stressful periods and times when looking out for their siblings.

Feeding flake and fresh frozen foods helps create a varied diet and thus in turn always ensuring your tropical fish have a healthy appetite and always eager to eat at feeding times.

Flake and Pellet foods are what I describe as clean foods and cause the least pollution in an aquarium when feeding. However with flake and pellet foods they are what they are, processed foods dried foods, where the natural water and juices have been removed from these foods.

Fresh frozen foods can be messy, but one fresh frozen food can vary to another. It is also important to note the consumption periods by the fish of frozen foods can vary. If your fish are keen eaters and enjoy the fresh frozen foods they will eat and digest these foods before they start to become a risk to the aquarium environment regarding any increase in aquarium pollution contaminants.

Fish, like all creatures and especially us as human beings, have a preference to certain food types. Even when feeding flake foods to tropical fish, some species in a community aquarium have a particular liking towards some parts of the food and not the other. When studying your fish at feeding times with flake food you can see that Tetras for example prefer parts of the flake food and guppies or platies for example like another part of the food.

It is very clear that the ingredients and formula when making flake foods is with the aim to accommodate most community aquarium tropical fish tastes and I might add, the dieticians developing these foods have done extremely well, for I never see any flake food uneaten or remaining after about 4 to 5 minutes.

When developing fresh frozen foods just as much thought and effort needs to go into the planning as commercial food dieticians to derive at the most suitable ingredients. I make my own fresh frozen foods even for my community aquarium fish inhabitants and these recipes are different to the fresh frozen foods planned and prepared for my Discus and Angel Fish for example.

The ingredients I use for my fresh frozen fish food for my community aquarium species includes; Broccoli, Spinach, Liver, Beef Heart, Prawns, Cods Roe and Beetroot for example and the addition of multi-vitamins. Now in the Book chapter for Feeding fish, you can find my recipes of fresh frozen fish foods that are markedly different regarding ingredients used for a recipe aimed at specific cichlids and again even variations in recipes for fish species age groups and stages of growth e.g. Junior and Adult Foods.

A staple Discus diet for example will only contain beef heart, spinach and beef liver in most cases. The grating size of the food also varies accordingly to growth of fish species in question. Larger fish species food is grated on a far coarser whereas younger species food is prepared by using a smaller grating setting.

Some fresh frozen foods may not be appealing at all to some fish species and this is another reason why when introducing a new fish food to the staple diet is to only feed very small amounts initially. Mysis or Sand Eels may be popular to some larger fish species of the characin family but not at all appealing to smaller members of the characin family such as tetras.

I have never found Mysis or Sand Eels to be very popular with many members of the Cichlid family and so initially it may be worth buying a small amount of a new fish food before acquiring any larger packets or containers.

Today as mentioned there is a large range of fish foods in the form of flake, freeze dried, pellet and fresh frozen on the market today.

Aquarists have a great choice available to them and many are worth trying to hopefully achieve the best results with regards to growth and wanting to breed.

Some foods you may find are not eagerly eaten and this I have found when feeding high protein foods for the very first time to fish not accustomed to the diet. When I bring in very young Discus occasionally to help in my program and to prevent inbreeding of the same family members for genetic reasons the young are never keen on the beef heart initially, but after about two days they cannot eat enough and then you have to be careful the fish do not overeat for fear of contracting the condition known as bloat.

New fish to the community aquarium may not initially be eager to eat your fish food that the rest of the inhabitants enjoy, this is normally as a result of the existing diet, where for example the retailer or shop owner has been feeding the fish just on bloodworm for ease due to the number of aquariums he or she has to maintain. Now bloodworms is a poplar food with most fish, but not the holy grail of food as fish do need a balanced diet just like us humans and most other creatures.

Another reason why new fish from a retailer may not be keen to eat is as a result of being rundown. The moving and disruption of any fish can be stressful and contrary to the myth of fish not remembering. Fish do remember and especially more evolved species such as cichlids and especially Discus, they can be very weary and mindful of disruption for many weeks. Some of my adult Discus fish look at me sometimes as if to say "what is he doing now" when I am carrying out some maintenance, or cleaning and they will literally sit in the water at the front of the aquarium watching me for as long as it takes.

Frozen Bloodworms are well worth including in your tropical fish's diet. Bloodworms are especially a valuable food source when trying to encourage fish to eat who have been suffering from being rundown. After a couple of weeks once you have managed to get your poorly fish eating again, is to start mixing in some flake food with the bloodworms, so eventually your poorly fish in question starts to enjoy a more balanced diet.

On a final note surrounding fish food products, is to always make sure you acquire these foods from a well-known trusted brand and producer.

Obviously if you are making your own fresh fish food for freezing, you are in control of the ingredients and therefore the well-being of your fish from the outset.

The secret to feeding any food is always little and often. If your fish species have an eager appetite simply feed them more times in a day. Adult Discus for example when coming into breeding will "eat you out of house and home" to coin a phrase when it comes to food and need to be fed 4 to 5 times a day.

Aquarium Products

Today when it comes to Aquariums in design and size, we are very much spoilt for choice, and a range of prices to meet every budget.

Throughout History in our pastime Engineering and Life Skills have played an important part and none more so than making our own Aquariums – Photograph by Alastair R Agutter

However there is another aspect to our pastime and hobby that has served us well over the decades and that has been Engineering and Life Skills, where many an Aquarium has been custom, or homemade.

Today unfortunately at this time glass is at a premium price due to demand in the solar panel industry. But for the best part of our hobby over the decades, the idea of making our own aquariums was always a viable option and idea. Thankfully at this time, there are still a good number of Glazier Shops in our communities and I am sure many would have some glass available for any aquarium project idea at a reasonable price.

When covering this section in the book on Aquariums it would be easy to list many great fish tank products and brands. But tropical fish keeping for me when I first started out in the hobby back in the 1960's is much more than just about products. For I think our hobby is just as importantly about people as well as our tropical fish and aquarium plants and from collective spirit and goodwill, we can see the very best in us all.

Just as gardening can get under your fingernails, Aquatics can get under your skin, and making your own aquarium is an experience and task well worth considering and undertaking if not now, perhaps in the future!

The name Aquarium was coined by the English Marine Biologist Philip Henry Gosse and built the first public aquarium in 1853 for London Zoo.

It was "The Great London Exhibition" of 1851 to 1853 that saw the hobby of tropical fish keeping really take off as fine ornamental cast iron aquariums were put on display by exhibitors.

Soon after "The Great London Exhibition" America and Germany entered the fray in Aquarium development, making aquariums from timber lined with pitch and glass fronts, angled iron aquariums made in glass with slate bottoms to heat aquariums from below.

Through the 20th Century aquarium design evolved with more robust steel welded angle frames that were enamel coated with glass panes lined by putty.

By the 1950's and 1960's, Aquarium design became works of art with ornate metal work and even bow fronted aquaria with more sophisticated enameling and anodizing or electro plating.

In the early part of the 1970's aquariums began to be constructed and made only from plate glass and using high modulus clear silicone sealants to bond the glass panes. Most common commercial sizes in those early days made with ¼ inch plate glass were; 24 x 12 x 12, 24 x 12 x 15, 36 x 12 x 15, 36 x 12 x 18, 48 x 12 x 15 and 48 x 12 x 18.

As confidence grew in this new design of all glass aquariums, larger custom designed aquariums were made using 3/8 inch plate glass and the most popular sizes were; 60 x 18 x 18, 60 x 18 x 24, 60 x 24 x 24, 72 x 18 x 18, 72 x 18 x 24 and 72 x 24 x 24.

Today even more sophisticated and larger designs of Aquariums exist made from acrylic and glass and in America, as you probably well know, even television programmes are now made and broadcast across the Discovery Channels on the subject.

The pastime of Tropical Fish Keeping I am pleased to say is growing yet again across Europe, Asia and North America. In fact, in the United States of America, tropical fish keeping is the biggest hobby after stamp collecting as reported in 1999.

If you would like to try your hand at making an aquarium, here are the following glass sizes for the aquarium in the picture at the start of this section. The silicone sealer required, can be easily obtained online and the full details of which are in the Chapter of Aquarium Sizes in the book.

Glass Sizes for a 36" x 18" x 21" Aquarium. All the glass is 6mm thick

1 @ 36" x 18" Base

2 @ 36" x 21" Sides

2 @ 21" x 17-1/2" Ends

2 @ 1-1/2" x 34" Side Ribs

2 @ 1-1/2" x 16" End Ribs

1 @ 3" x 16" Centre Rib

Energy Lighting Solutions for Your Aquarium

Today aquarium lighting comes in many styles and thankfully each day more designs are becoming more energy efficient.

One of the Author's Naturally Planted Aquariums using Energy Efficient Lighting that comes with a 10 year life product guarantee – Photograph by Alastair R Agutter

The history of lighting is very rarely ever covered in literature and is a fascinating area of the pastime for early forms of lighting for aquariums started with gas light elements often found in a home and where an aquarium was strategically placed below such a fixture. At the beginning of the 20th century (1900's) the humble light bulb began to be used for the illumination of aquariums. Eventually light bulbs began to be housed in aquarium hoods, as aquarium designs further advanced with the use of angle iron steel metals and light gauge aluminium used for aquarium hoods.

Fluorescent lighting was unleashed onto the World at "The World's Fair Exhibition in 1939" and a few years later rope lighting as it was known was soon finding its way into the World of Aquatics and still continues to be used today as white light and Grolux.

Regarding commercial aquariums today and their lighting, many or most of the fish tanks come with built in lighting systems that are either fluorescent or LED.

The lighting used for one of my naturally planted aquariums pictured above, is from green energy efficient lighting products that have a 10 year guarantee. The actual bulbs have on average a power output of between 75 to 100 watts per each bulb, but is in fact only between 15 to 20 watts in size.

Spotlights and Halogen (Mercury Vapour) Lights are an ever increasing popular choice today with many Aquarists. These light systems are normally suspended above the aquarium from wall mounts or hanging from the ceiling.

Always remember fish like routine and so the investment in a timer switch for your lighting will always be a worthwhile investment and appreciated by your fish. Remember that the lighting period needs to be between 10 to 12 hours and the actual wattage of the lighting for the size of your aquarium can be found in the reference tables chapter.

UV Sterilization:

In this section of products and accessories as promised in the book, I said I would cover for Aquarists valuable information surrounding UV Sterilization, Reverse Osmosis and Deionization.

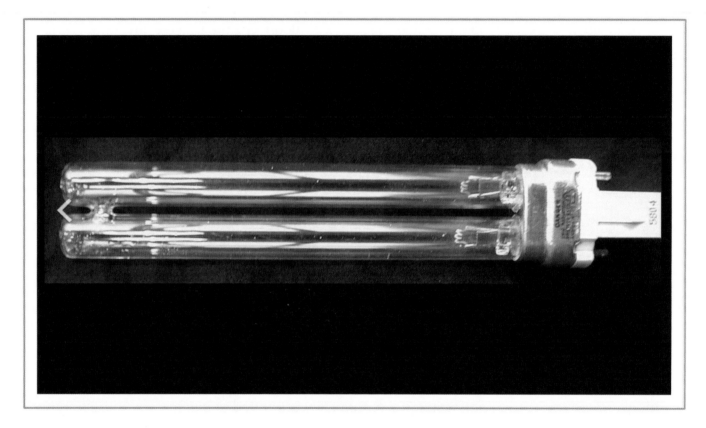

Germicidal UV Lamp in a Fluorescent Tube Unit – Photograph Courtesy of Wikipedia (Creative Commons License Permissions) and Artwork Compiled by Alastair R Agutter

I have always been a great advocate for technology and human advancement, but with a rational and balanced approach, for the more we study Natural Law in the fields of Quantum Mechanics and Natural Branching a greater appreciation is attained regarding every element we believe we know and pretend to understand.

You see we need to understand the big picture and this far extends beyond this Earth. All the time we have space and other planets that do include and house life, we need to have a constantly evolving resistant immune system to meet these changes and this can be said for all other life forms we have come to love and know who we share this small planet with.

Perhaps in a 100 or 1000 years, humankind will understand and it will be commonly known that all that we know is connected, and where this is especially relevant to seeding.

Every species on the planet from Quantum Mechanics and Natural Branching is continually advancing and this extends to microbiology and immunity.

UV Sterilization is what it is and that is a method of disinfectant of any form of microbial life forms. UV sterilization units I deem to be a lazy form of aquarium maintenance but with a contradiction. For one of the key elements in water quality is a fully functioning biological bacterial filtration system.

The presence of UV Sterilization in any form will inhibit or eliminate any bacterial activity that is critical to breaking down waste matter and oxides in the aquarium's water.

UV Sterilization can and will over time weaken the immune system of fish inhabitant species. A strong immune system in fish is the barrier to fend off and threatening bacterial infections or more prominent diseases.

If we took a very close look at our own bodies under a microscope you will find that our bodies are alive with bacterial activity and micro-organisms.

Our very own atmosphere is alive with activity and as we know is the common method of contracting colds and other viruses. Water is no different and airborne alien entities in the form of viruses do descend into the depths of our Marine World.

Scientists are today now beginning to understand where there is any form of moisture or water, micro-organisms can be carried, and this includes meteors, or asteroids, that are now being seriously considered with regards to how life was first established on Earth.

If we look closer to home with regards to Earth, every species on the planet does serve a purpose and if we equated Earth to an evolving formula one engine, we would immediately know that every component is essential for the motor to work and perform.

It is from climate change that I warned about over 25 years ago in my first tropical fish book that clearly demonstrates today how our performance engine of Earth is now starting to malfunction as components are removed in the form of animal and plant life species.

So regarding UV Sterilization, it is no friend to any form of Marine Life or environment we seek to maintain or replicate.

Reverse Osmosis

Another method of water purification I hear about is Reverse Osmosis and in truth most of these methods discussed in tropical fish magazines, or by others, I describe as Techno-geek Aquarists, is another method and technology that is dangerous to an aquarium environment and the ideas of use by such authors or columnists, indicates to me a total lack of any in-depth knowledge of our pastime.

Reverse Osmosis is a process of forcing a liquid through a filtration method, this being water through a semi-permeable membrane, a fine mesh in other words. The process is enabled by forcing the liquid through to eliminate metal trace elements, salts, minerals, calcium's and even microbial entities and bacteria.

Now to aid this process of reverse osmosis, chemicals can be used to assist this process, sounds familiar, with regards to fracking. To then deliver at the other end of the process a sterile liquid with a very low general hardness (DH or GH).

Keeping, rearing and breeding any fish species successfully is achieved by a few simple rules.

- 1/. An abundance of water (on tap)
- 2/. High Protein Healthy Foods
- 3/. Correct Lighting
- 4/. Lastly, a Routine

If Aquarists abide by these key rules above and with a regime of regular care and maintenance, there will never be a need for additional man-made products that in truth constitute as being dangerous gimmicks.

This method can only really be of used on large scale State Region waterways where the water is so polluted nothing is able to survive. This is where Reverse Osmosis treatment plants can begin a process to purify water. But then even after that process, various metal and trace elements have to be re-introduced back into the water, to begin and start the long process of establishing natural plant and marine animal life forms once again.

Deionization

Today there are a number of processes for developing deionized water to remove minerals, anions (chlorides), copper, iron, sulphate etc. The aim of which is to lower the General Hardness (DH or GH) of Water so it becomes a purer liquid a good example being battery water.

One process is to use electrodes to remove metal trace elements and another is to again force water through a series of pipes housing ion-exchange resins that are normally microbeads to collect and trap the minerals, metals, salts etc.

The process is very long and laborious to produce small amounts of deionized water and also this process does not remove bacteria and other microbial organisms. Deionizers when not in use, such systems can in fact create a build-up of bacterial organisms from the moisture retained in these tube systems. Flushing is very often recommended but in truth how much flushing is required before you know the system is safe.

I will be honest as always and this is based on experience of using Deionizers as part of an experiment over 25 years ago when trying to breed Discus in captivity.

The deionized process could never produce enough water for me, as I had a requirement of water changes per week in excess of 450 gallons and these units on average were only capable of producing around a 120 litres (27 UK imperial gallons) at best, before cleaning and flushing, or replacing in some instances.

Deionized water is without doubt extremely useful in the medical profession and pharmaceutical industry, but not practical when it comes to keeping healthy thriving tropical fish. For one thing tropical fish need is routine and consistency. The great secret in breeding regarding water, is to get your tropical fish acclimatized to your local water, so then it is "on tap" to coin a phrase, so then you can carry out as many water changes as you wish and as often as you want.

IMPORTANT: Microbeads are soon to be banned, as they are a man-made substance pollutant now finding their way into the food chain (your tropical fish) at a dangerous level globally.

Regarding some commercial products and technology available today for the Aquarist such as; Deionizers, Reverse Osmosis and UV Sterilizers for tropical fish keeping. I think we need to sometimes step back and see things for what they truly are and in this instance, these products are nothing other than a commercial opportunity.

I am constantly reminding Students, Academia and the Public, in our Global Society, that the more we supposedly advance, the "window for error" becomes forever smaller. Very often we think we know, but then there is that old saying from time and memorial "where fools rush in."

Today from our naïve commercial world of miracle face creams and other cosmetics, all our Oceans, Estuaries, Rivers, Streams and Lakes are now under serious threat from microbeads, that are being digested by Marine Life and also polluting the water and finding their way into every part of the food table, regarding everything we eat.

Even Fowl and Farm Animals affected, as these are fed at some time intensive enriched pellet foods, containing fish meal in some form.

Accessories

In this last part of the products and accessories section I have written some summaries about some useful items often used or referred too for further helping the tropical fish hobbyist and dedicated aquarist.

1/. Cable Tidy Unit 2/. Polyatomic-ion Biological Reactor 3/. Condensation Tray 4/. Air Stone and Valve 5/. Heater Thermostats, Air Pump and Fish Food 6/. Powerhead 7/. Books 8/. Undergravel Filter – Photographs by Alastair R Agutter

Cable Tidy

This product is freely available and helps greatly to tidy up all those aquarium cables. The units normally allow the aquarist to connect heater thermostats, lighting and pumps.

Biological Filters

With Biological Filters today, you will find there are many types of filtration on the market today, the Polyatomic-ion Biological Reactor that I have developed is easy to make and assemble for delivering crystal clear water.

Condensation Trays

Condensation Trays ar still used today in many instances even though many new aquariums today come with condensation trays normally in the form of light gauge sliding glass or polycarbonate panes or panels. But conventional aquariums such as all glass, or built by you for a project, or fish house, will require condensation trays. These condensation trays can be easily obtained from your tropical fish or pet store. But what I use very often as condensation trays and as a cost saving exercise are the trays from the supermarkets that meat is sold in. These trays are ideal once washed and when the remainder of the thin plastic film is removed.

Air Stones

Air Stones are frequently used to deliver more air to an aquarium, I tend to use them especially in rearing and breeding fish tanks towards the surface of the aquarium to encourage and help fish growth.

Air Valves

Air Valves are always a useful piece of equipment used between an Air Pump and filter or air stone to regulate the delivery of air to the device in question. More fashionable and better made vales are available today made form metal and with a greater regulating method.

Heater Thermostats

With Heater Thermostats always remember to ensure all heater thermostats are fitted with 3 Amp Plugs for safety reasons. Heater thermostats normally come in sizes ranging from 50 to 300 watt to heat various sizes of fish tanks.

Air Pumps

Air Pumps are still very popular and more energy efficient today and a lot quieter compared to air pumps over past decades. Their purpose is to deliver air to filters and air stones etc. Again always ensure this device is fitted with a 3 Amp plug for safety reasons.

Flake Foods

Flake Foods are a very popular fish food that forms part of a staple diet for most tropical fish. But always ensure you vary the diet and include high protein fresh frozen foods also to encourage healthy thriving fish and growth.

Powerheads

Powerheads are often used today on uplifts of under gravel filters (not recommended) and for biological sumps, reservoirs and trickle filters successfully.

Books

Books I know today the World Wide Web can offer a mass of information, but many tropical fish books carry valuable information compiled very often over many years by known competent and knowledgeable aquarists. The trouble taken to write and produce such book's, is testament to the measure of importance placed on the subject matter by the aquarists author.

Undergravel Filters

Undergravel Filters are still used in many aquariums today, I personally do not use them, as you can create a build-up of toxins and matter in the substrate that is not broken down successfully, as a result of little, or no plat life, as undergravel filters do damage plant root systems and therefore inhibits any plant growth.

Aquarists Reference Tables

In this section of the Tropical Fish Keeping Journal are the essential tables as a reference for all aquarists and tropical fish hobbyists. This series of tables will help Aquarists find information and answers quickly, and I hope they will be an invaluable constant point of reference.

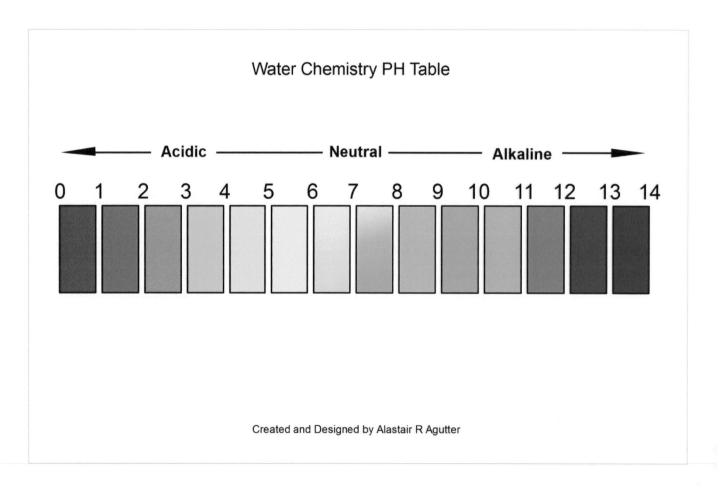

Diagram of the PH Table from 0 to 14 – Created and Designed by Alastair R Agutter

This table above shows the water hardness and softness range, so Aquarists can quickly reference PH levels regarding their own local tap and aquarium water.

The PH table also shows what I describe as the "Goldey-Locks" range of 6.0 to 8.0 PH that is an inhabitable water quality for most species of tropical fish.

Water Hardness DH Table

PPM CaCo3	DH	Conditioning
20 40 60	1.12 2.25 3.37	Soft
80 100	4.49 5.61	Moderately Soft
140 180	7.87 10.11	Ideal
220 260	12.36 14.61	Hard
300	16.85	Very Hard

Created and Designed by Alastair R Agutter

Diagram of the General Hardness Table – Created and Designed by Alastair R Agutter

This table above shows the general hardness (GH or DH) of water, so Aquarists can quickly reference DH levels regarding their own local tap and aquarium water.

The DH or GH table provides an insight to the amount of salts and minerals found in the Aquarists water, as some species can be sensitive to metals and calcium's in the water with regards to reproduction. Some species include Discus, Angel Fish, Hatchet Fish, Cardinal and Neon Tetras.

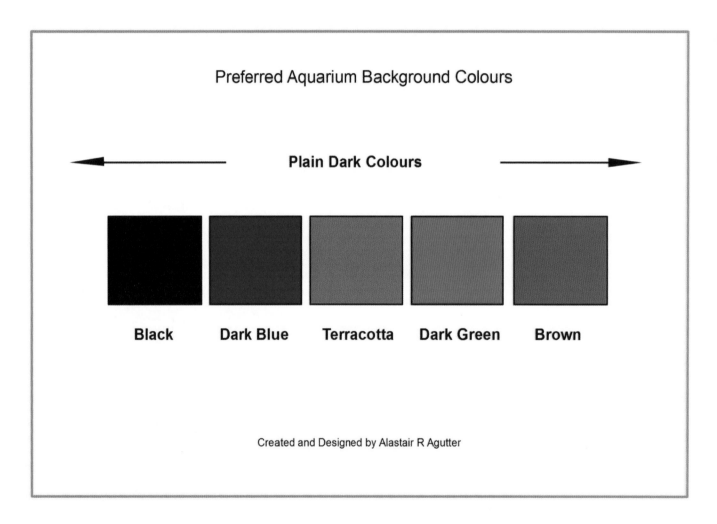

Diagram of Aquarium Backgrounds Table – Created and Designed by Alastair R Agutter

This table above shows the preferred background colours of Aquariums as this does have a significant bearing on fish species colours and desire for breeding.

Background colours are also important for fish species well-being as they can become stressed from background colours and patterns that can disorientate fish species, as they function with the use of electromagnetic energies and waves to map out their environment and can see in full colour like human beings.

Black, Terracotta and Dark Green are particularly favourable colours for fish species to bring out their colour and for breeding. But also these colours are favourable background colours for enhancing aquatic plants and ornate objects such as bogwoods.

Biological Bacteria Volume Mass Diagram

Fish Units	Temperature	BBVM's	Filter Flow Rate
5	78	40 BBVM	10 Gallons
5	84	55 BBVM	10 Gallons
10	78	80 BBVM	15 Gallons
10	84	110 BBVM	15 Gallons
15	78	120 BBVM	20 Gallons
15	84	165 BBVM	20 Gallons
20	78	160 BBVM	25 Gallons
20	84	220 BBVM	25 Gallons
Per Unit	Fahrenheit	Per Million	Gallons

Created and Designed by Alastair R Agutter

Diagram of Bacteria Volume Mass Table – Created and Designed by Alastair R Agutter

This table above shows the biological bacteria volume mass in Aquariums at certain temperature levels in relation to the number of fish species being housed and the volume of water processed as a filtration rate in gallons.

Tropical fish species in an aquarium requires the biological breakdown process of fish bye products and therefore a bacterial population culture has to exist.

Established aquariums can only be established if fish exist to allow for the populating of the bacteria that breaks down and eats the waste products of the fish and in a naturally planted aquarium, the breakdown of plant waste in the form of deteriorating leaves etc.

No chemicals can accelerate this process as it is a natural chemical phenomenon of nature populating polyatomic-ions in the form of oxides these being mainly Ammonia, Nitrite and Nitrates.

Aquarium Sizes For Number of Fish Inhabitants Table

Aquarium Size	Cubic Inches of Fish	Aquarium Size	Cubic Inches of Fish
18" x 12" x 12"	18 inches of fish	48" x 12" x 15"	60 inches of fish
24" x 12" x 15"	25 inches of fish	48" x 12" x 18"	72 inches of fish
24" x 12" x 18"	30 inches of fish	48" x 18" x 18"	108 inches of fish
24" x 24" x 24"	48 inches of fish	48" x 18" x 24"	144 inches of fish
30" x 12" x 15"	37 inches of fish	60" x 12" x 18"	75 inches of fish
30" x 12" x 18"	45 inches of fish	60" x 18" x 18"	135 inches of fish
36" x 12" x 15"	35 inches of fish	60" x 18" x 24"	180 inches of fish
36" x 12" x 18"	54 inches of fish	72" x 18" x 18"	162 inches of fish
36" x 18" x 18"	81 inches of fish	72" x 18" x 24"	216 inches of fish

Created and Designed by Alastair R Agutter

Diagram of Aquarium Sizes and Number of Fish – Created and Designed by Alastair R Agutter

This table above shows the size of aquariums and the number of fish that can be comfortably housed.

It is important to have such a reference to ensure fish inhabitant species can grow successfully when the correct numbers of fish are being housed.

When aquarists overstock aquariums there is a greater risk of disease and deformity in the fish from stunted growth.

Also, when there is a too heavy population of fish in an aquarium, there is a high risk of bacterial build-up and explosions, again causing fish to lose their appetite and exposed to disease as a result of the water conditions caused.

Aquarium Sizes and Optimal Filter Flow Rates Table

Aquarium Size	Filter Flow Rate	Aquarium Size	Filter Flow Rate
18" x 12" x 12"	11.55 Litres per hour	48" x 12" x 15"	38.50 Litres per hour
24" x 12" x 15"	19.25 Litres per hour	48" x 12" x 18"	46.20 Litres per hour
24" x 12" x 18"	23.10 Litres per hour	48" x 18" x 18"	69.30 Litres per hour
24" x 24" x 24"	61.60 Litres per hour	48" x 18" x 24"	92.40 Litres per hour
30" x 12" x 15"	24.02 Litres per hour	60" x 12" x 18"	57.75 Litres per hour
30" x 12" x 18"	28.87 Litres per hour	60" x 18" x 18"	86.62 Litres per hour
36" x 12" x 15"	28.87 Litres per hour	60" x 18" x 24"	115.50 Litres per hour
36" x 12" x 18"	34.65 Litres per hour	72" x 18" x 18"	103.95 Litres per hour
36" x 18" x 18"	51.97 Litres per hour	72" x 18" x 24"	138.60 Litres per hour

Created and Designed by Alastair R Agutter

Aquarium Sizes and Filtration Flow Rates – Created and Designed by Alastair R Agutter

Aquarium sizes and optimal filtration flow rates per hour are not often covered in any detail, but they are very important and critical if you are seeking an optimal aquarium with healthy thriving fish.

This diagram helps you to refer to popular aquarium sizes to establish the flow rate for your aquarium. Most filtration products in the form of air pumps or powerhead units today provide information of the litre output capacity and ability. With some simple calculations you can establish your needs with the help of this table.

When flow rates are too high through a filtration unit, very often waste material is passed through the biological bacterial culture housed inside the filtration system too fast, resulting in the failure to breakdown the material properly. The re-cycling of waste material in the aquarium causes a bacterial build-up in the fish tank and often reported cloudy water.

Heater Thermostats Wattage and Aquarium Sizes Table

Aquarium Size	Heater Thermostats	Aquarium Size	Heater Thermostats
18" x 12" x 12"	1 x 100 watt	48" x 12" x 15"	2 x 100 watt
24" x 12" x 15"	1 x 150 watt	48" x 12" x 18"	2 x 150 watt
24" x 12" x 18"	1 x 150 watt	48" x 18" x 18"	2 x 200 watt
24" x 24" x 24"	1 x 300 watt	48" x 18" x 24"	2 x 200 watt
30" x 12" x 15"	1 x 150 watt	60" x 12" x 18"	2 x 200 watt
30" x 12" x 18"	1 x 200 watt	60" x 18" x 18"	2 x 200 watt
36" x 12" x 15"	1 x 200 watt	60" x 18" x 24"	2 x 300 watt
36" x 12" x 18"	1 x 200 watt	72" x 18" x 18"	2 x 300 watt
36" x 18" x 18"	1 x 300 watt	72" x 18" x 24"	2 x 300 watt

Created and Designed by Alastair R Agutter

Heater Thermostat Wattage and Aquarium Sizes – Created and Designed by Alastair R Agutter

I hope this table also provides help and assists with regards to establishing the correct size of heater thermostat and wattage output for your aquarium.

All heater thermostat commercial products indicate the actual size of the device, but little is often written or covered with regards to the actual size or number of heater thermostats required for specific aquarium water volume mass in relation to gallons and litres.

These sizes of heater thermostats in the form of wattage are based on an average atmospheric temperature amongst Countries in winter and summer seasons. If you come from a region where the weather is extremely cold, well then you may need to increase this wattage as the aquarium's water battles with the external elements. If for example your weather is extreme temperature wise, well then purchase a 150 watt heater thermostat instead of a 100 watt heater thermostat.

Lighting Wattage and Aquarium Sizes Table

Aquarium Size	Lighting Wattage	Aquarium Size	Lighting Wattage
18" x 12" x 12"	100 watts	48" x 12" x 15"	300 watts
24" x 12" x 15"	100 watts	48" x 12" x 18"	300 watts
24" x 12" x 18"	100 watts	48" x 18" x 18"	300 watts
24" x 24" x 24"	200 watts	48" x 18" x 24"	300 watts
30" x 12" x 15"	150 watts	60" x 12" x 18"	350 watts
30" x 12" x 18"	150 watts	60" x 18" x 18"	350 watts
36" x 12" x 15"	200 watts	60" x 18" x 24"	350 watts
36" x 12" x 18"	200 watts	72" x 18" x 18"	400 watts
36" x 18" x 18"	200 watts	72" x 18" x 24"	400 watts

Created and Designed by Alastair R Agutter

Lighting Wattage and Aquarium Sizes Table – Created and Designed by Alastair R Agutter

Aquarium lighting in a naturally planted aquarium is especially important for the successful growth of your aquarium plants but also your fish regarding their growth and body bone development.

This table shows the correct aquarium wattage I have researched that works and with a lighting period of time each day being between 10 to 12 hours.

As you know fish like routine and so even the switching on and off of the aquarium lights can be achieved with the help of a plug, or wall unit timer set to 10 to 12 hours a day, starting at time A and ending at time B.

The failure to regulate the correct times and wattage of light in an aquarium will result in plant deterioration and this can be very quickly over a matter of a few days and weeks, leading to unwanted excessive numbers of toxins (pollution) building up in the aquarium.

Aquarium UK Gallons to Litres Table

Aquarium Size	UK Gallons	Litres	Aquarium Size	UK Gallons	Litres
18" x 12" x 12"	9.34	42.42	48" x 12" x 15"	31.15	141.42
24" x 12" x 15"	12.46	56.56	48" x 12" x 18"	37.38	169.70
24" x 12" x 18"	18.69	82.23	48" x 18" x 18"	56.07	254.55
24" x 24" x 24"	49.84	226.27	48" x 18" x 24"	74.76	339.41
30" x 12" x 15"	20.24	91.88	60" x 12" x 18"	46.72	212.10
30" x 12" x 18"	23.36	106.05	60" x 18" x 18"	70.08	318.16
36" x 12" x 15"	23.36	106.05	60" x 18" x 24"	93.45	424.26
36" x 12" x 18"	28.03	127.25	72" x 18" x 18"	84.10	381.81
36" x 18" x 18"	42.05	190.90	72" x 18" x 24"	112.14	509.11

Created and Designed by Alastair R Agutter

Aquarium UK Gallons to Litres Table – Created and Designed by Alastair R Agutter

Above is a conversion table of UK Imperial Gallons converted to Litres and these are accompanied with the most common aquarium sizes. No do not despair if your aquarium is not listed as the following mathematical formula will help you determine the actual size of your aquarium.

First measure the length of your aquarium, its depth and finally height. This being L x W x H then multiply these in inches to acquire the mathematical total to the equation. Example 30 x 15 x 15 = 6750, then divide into 6750 the figure of 1728 (cubic square foot in inches) and this will provide a total of 3.906 and this figure is the cubic square feet of this aquarium example. Then multiply the cubic feet of 3.90 by 6.23 (UK) gallons. This then gives you a total figure of 3.90 x 6.23 =

24.29. Then finally multiply the UK Gallons of 24.29 x 4.54 which equals 110.30 and this figure is the litres of this aquarium converted from UK Imperial Gallons.

Aquarium US Gallons to Litres Table

Aquarium Size	US Gallons	Litres	Aquarium Size	US Gallons	Litres
18" x 12" x 12"	11.22	42.10	48" x 12" x 15"	37.40	141.37
24" x 12" x 15"	14.96	56.54	48" x 12" x 18"	44.88	169.64
24" x 12" x 18"	22.44	84.82	48" x 18" x 18"	67.32	254.46
24" x 24" x 24"	62.24	235.26	48" x 18" x 24"	59.84	226.19
30" x 12" x 15"	24.31	91.89	60" x 12" x 18"	56.10	212.05
30" x 12" x 18"	28.05	106.02	60" x 18" x 18"	84.15	318.08
36" x 12" x 15"	28.05	106.02	60" x 18" x 24"	112.20	424.11
36" x 12" x 18"	33.66	127.23	72" x 18" x 18"	100.98	381.70
36" x 18" x 18"	50.49	190.85	72" x 18" x 24"	134.64	511.63

Created and Designed by Alastair R Agutter

Aquarium US Gallons to Litres Table – Created and Designed by Alastair R Agutter

Above is a conversion table of US Imperial Gallons converted to Litres and these are accompanied with the most common aquarium sizes. No do not despair if your aquarium is not listed as the following mathematical formula will help you determine the actual size of your aquarium.

First measure the length of your aquarium, its depth and finally height. This being L x W x H then multiply these in inches to acquire the mathematical total to the equation. Example 30 x 15 x 15 = 6750, then divide into 6750 the figure of 1728 (cubic square foot in inches) and this will provide a total of 3.906 and this figure is the cubic square feet of this aquarium example. Then multiply the cubic feet of 3.90 by 7.48 (US) gallons. This then gives you a total figure of 3.90 x 7.48 = 24.17. Then finally multiply the US Gallons of 24.17 x 3.78 which equals 91.36 litres and this figure is the litres of this aquarium example converted from US Imperial Gallons.

Aquarium Sizes to Cubic Square Feet Table

Aquarium Size	Cubic Square Feet	Aquarium Size	Cubic Square Feet
18" x 12" x 12"	1.5 Cu Sq ft	48" x 12" x 15"	5.0 Cu Sq ft
24" x 12" x 15"	2.5 Cu Sq ft	48" x 12" x 18"	6.0 Cu Sq ft
24" x 12" x 18"	3.0 Cu Sq ft	48" x 18" x 18"	9.0 Cu Sq ft
24" x 24" x 24"	8.0 Cu Sq ft	48" x 18" x 24"	12.0 Cu Sq ft
30" x 12" x 15"	3.25 Cu Sq ft	60" x 12" x 18"	7.5 Cu Sq ft
30" x 12" x 18"	3.75 Cu Sq ft	60" x 18" x 18"	11.25 Cu Sq ft
36" x 12" x 15"	3.75 Cu Sq ft	60" x 18" x 24"	15.00 Cu Sq ft
36" x 12" x 18"	4.50 Cu Sq ft	72" x 18" x 18"	13.50 Cu Sq ft
36" x 18" x 18"	6.75 Cu Sq ft	72" x 18" x 24"	18.0 Cu Sq ft

Created and Designed by Alastair R Agutter

Aquarium Sizes to Cubic Square Feet Table – Created and Designed by Alastair R Agutter

This table provides the Cubic Square Feet measurement of a number of aquarium sizes listed above. The Cubic Square Feet of Aquariums is obviously important in tropical fish keeping regarding a whole host of subject areas covered and where very often you may find yourself in need of the aquarium Cubic Square Foot size. Relevant areas that come to mind as a few examples are; Amount of Gallons or Litres, for Medication purposes and heating with reference to heater thermostat wattage requirements.

If your aquarium is not listed above do not despair as I will now take you through a simple mathematical formula that will allow you to establish the Cubic Square Foot capacity of any aquarium.

Simply multiply the L x W x H of the aquarium in inches and then divided the total figure by 1728.

This will then provide you with the Cubic Square Feet of the Aquarium in question.

Here is a following example for you:-

I have an aquarium that is 40 inches in length, a depth or width of 20 inches and a height of 18 inches.

So, if I multiply 40 x 20 x 18 this figure total equals = 14400. Now if I divide 14400 by 1728 it gives me a figure of 8.333 and this total figure is in fact the Cubic Square Feet of the above aquarium example.

Now if for medical or filter purposes I need to know how many gallons this represents in UK imperial gallons, I simply multiply 8.33 which is the cubic square feet of the aquarium itself by 6.23 that is the UK gallons found in one cubic square foot and so the total of UK gallons for this aquarium equals 51.91 UK Gallons.

Now if I need my gallons to be in Litres!

I simply multiply 51.91 UK Gallons by 4.54 and this will give me the number of Litres in the Aquarium and this being 235.70.

I hope in this chapter I have covered all the tables required for our pastime of tropical fish keeping and where they are together, so they are easier to find as a quick reference.

Aquarists Book Guide

A selection of Tropical Fish Hobbyist Books and Magazines as essential reading, written by Best Selling Author Alastair R Agutter who Celebrating 50 years' experience (1967 to 2017) as an Aquarist.

Tropical Fish Keeping Journal Edition Book One

In this issue of the **"Tropical Fish Keeping Journal"** book edition one, we cover; the history of tropical fish keeping and the unmistakable contribution made by our Victorian Ancestors. Helping new aquarists get started. Choosing the correct themes and styles for the aquarist's planned aquarium(s). Choosing the right sized fish tank, including the supporting stand required for the job and the importance of positioning the aquarium in the right place.

My First Aquarium Book

My First Aquarium – The Joy of Tropical Fish Keeping is a book for all new and existing aquarists participating in the noble and time honoured traditional pastime of tropical fish keeping.

The Best Selling Author of Tropical Fish Keeping shares his knowledge of five decades since taking up the hobby in 1967 with you for keeping healthy thriving tropical fish and as one of the World's select few to successfully breed wild Discus in captivity over 25 years ago the king of the tropical fish aquarium.

Inside this book are over 390 pages of valuable information, containing over 93,000 plus words and over 250 plus photographs, diagrams and illustrations to ensure every aquarist is successful in their life's journey of tropical fish keeping.

The Discus Book 1st Edition

The Discus Book First Edition for the Dedicated Aquarist and a continue Best Selling Book now for 28 years since first being published in 1989.

The Discus Book is an invaluable reference book, for all Tropical Fish Keepers and Hobbyists, seeking to know more for successfully breeding Discus the King of the Aquarium and enjoying healthy, happy, thriving tropical fish free of disease.

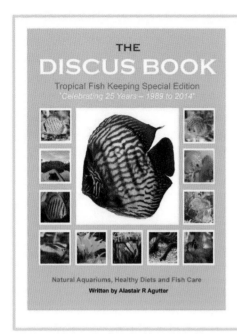 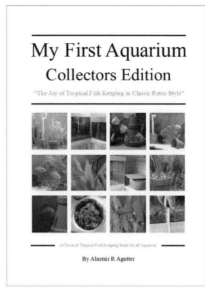 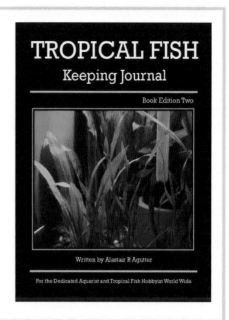

The Discus Book Tropical Fish Keeping Special Edition

The original "The Discus Book" was first published in 1989 and still remains a Best Seller world-wide even today and a classic collector's edition. Since then and 25 years later, "The Discus Book Tropical Fish Keeping Special Edition" celebrates 25 years in 2014 as a full colour special edition. With over 110 full colour pictures and just 17 black and white images of early days spanning 25 years as a special edition book.

This Book is for all Tropical Fish Hobbyists and enthusiasts. You will find inside the book, proven methods for the successful keeping of any tropical fish, always healthy and disease free, but especially Discus (symphysodon).

This "Special Edition" is suitable for all Tropical Fish Keeping enthusiasts of all ages. With a blaze of fabulous colour plates and pictures, including images and photographs from the breeders first book 25 years ago as mentioned earlier in the description, and now these archive images serve as a time capsule in book form, for every Aquarist to study, reminisce and enjoy!

This book covers; Fish Care for Discus, Cichlids and other Tropical Fish species. Natural Aquariums, Successful Breeding of Cichlids, Community Fish Aquariums, Filtration, Lighting, Suitable Plants, Special Recipes in the book for Preparing High Protein Fish Food to ensure your tropical fish are always healthy and thriving.

My First Aquarium Collector's Edition

My First Aquarium Collector's Edition Book – "The Joy of Tropical Fish Keeping in Classic Retro Style"

Taking up the noble and time honoured traditional pastime of tropical fish keeping should be an enjoyable experience for all. This book will become a valuable companion and friend to all new and existing aquarists, seeking the right advice and answers, to chart and navigate a successful path and journey for years to come!

This same journey began for the author back in 1967, five decades ago, and today he is just as passionate about the hobby and pastime as he was then. Sharing 50 years of knowledge, and as folk know, hands-on experience counts!

Tropical Fish Keeping Journal Book Edition Two

In book edition two of the **"Tropical Fish Keeping Journal"** we cover; the choice of aquarium substrates and their advantages. Successfully growing and keeping aquatic plants for the naturally planted aquarium. Different filtration methods and systems for the aquarium, to achieve the very best results for safe crystal clear water.

  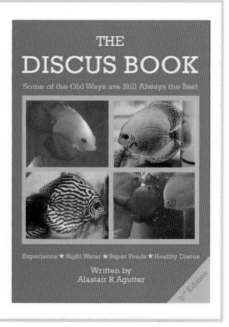

Super Foods Tropical Fish and Discus Book

Make your own Tropical Fish and Discus Cichlids Super Foods and See Your Healthy, Happy Thriving Fish Growing by the Day!

In the book, you will find a great number of fabulous super food recipes to try for your tropical fish and discus. I know by using any of these recipes, you will eventually have healthy, happy, thriving tropical fish, and growing to a size you could have only imagined.

Tropical Fish Keeping Journal Book Edition Three

In book edition three of the "Tropical Fish Keeping Journal" we cover; water quality and conditions, to the techniques, products and methods to heating the tropical fish aquarium, to lighting systems and the choices available for the aquarist and a little history, to finally fish behaviour and physiology.

The Discus Book 2nd Edition

This Second Edition of The Discus Book has been written and produced with updates and additional information since the first edition, written in 1989, to accommodate "some" of the questionable technology changes, regarding this species since the first edition of the Discus Book, when the Author successfully bred Wild Discus (symphysodon) in captivity, the recording of such work and events transcribed to the said printed book.

Alastair Agutter still remains one of a select few in the world today to accomplish such a feat, breeding wild symphysodon, and as a result of such endeavours by he, and other dedicated Aquarist colleagues, they managed to break a cycle and taboo that had lasted for more than 120 years, since the founding of the pastime we know as tropical fish keeping, after "The Great Exhibition" of 1851 and this being, to breed "The King of the Aquarium" in captivity.

This second edition of the book is concise and accurate, based on proven methods and techniques, to deliver the above results. The Discus, King of the Aquarium is a highly evolved species of the Cichlidae (tooth carp) Family and will challenge any Aquarist, even tank bred species. This book will not produce any quick fixes, or silver bullets to keeping symphysodon, whom are a very highly evolved sensitive species. But will provide the secrets to successfully keeping the species, if the valuable information found in this book is followed to the letter.

Der Diskus Buch

Das Discus-Buch ist ein unschätzbares Nachschlagewerk für alle Tropical Fish Keepers und Hobbyisten, um mehr für die erfolgreiche Zucht Discus den König des Aquariums zu erfahren und gesunde, glückliche, blühende tropische Fische frei von Krankheiten zu genießen.

Gardening for Beginners

Gardening for Beginners Book is a fabulous gift for friends, family and loved ones of any age seeking to take up the free and healthy pastime of Horticulture.

As we become more aware of our environment and wild life, with this book you can take the plunge of creating a mini eco-system around your home for a healthier lifestyle and creating a blaze of colour. Blooming Marvellous!

The book comes with many great gardening ideas including the growing of your own organic vegetables for healthier eating and giving new life to items around your home that can be recycled and given a new lease of life as part of the garden landscape. Also a new lease of life for yourself, with healthy free exercise, ensuring a healthier lifestyle, and remaining in good health, both physically and mentally.

Gardening for Beginners has been 2 years in the making by Alastair R Agutter Best Selling author of specialist books and found within this publication only encouragement with step by step guides and many great ideas for making your home into a little piece of Eden.

The Complete Angler and Master Rod Maker

Izaak Walton himself was a consummate angler in between the profession and teachings of the Church and where there can be found in many anglers, a deep connection of enlightenment from fishing. For the many who pursue such a noble pastime, are often great philosophers, for they are at their most peaceful and given time to think and ponder with their maker.

I often say angling is where you can unite yourself again with nature and rejuvenate the soul. There is no finer thing, than to be surrounded by the picturesque canvas of nature and to witness from sight, such beauty and from God's gift of hearing, become inspired from the vibrant life of nature's fellow creatures.

Aquarists Directory

Welcome to the Aquarists Directory for useful resources and suppliers related to our tropical fish keeping pastime.

Eheim Aquatics

Eheim: World renowned leading German manufacturers, and makers of fine Aquarium Equipment, including Canister Filters for over 56 years.
Web Site: https://www.eheim.com/

Fluval Aquatics

Fluval Aquatics: Well-known manufacturers and makers of Aquarium products including Canister Filters.
Web Site: www.fluvalaquatics.com/

Tetra Aquatic Products

Tetra: Leading Manufacturers of Aquariums, Fish Foods and Tropical Fish Keeping Accessories including Fish Care Products.
Web Site: http://www.tetra-fish.com/

King British Flake Foods

King British: Manufacturers of Fish Foods, Water Treatments and Aquatic Medicines.
Web Site: www.kingbritish.co.uk/

Juwel Aquariums

Juwel Aquariums: Manufacturers and Makers of Quality Aquariums and Accessories.
Web Site: www.juwel-aquarium.co.uk

BiOrb Aquariums

BiOrb Aquariums: Makers and Manufacturers of Custom Design Aquariums and Accessories.

Web Site: http://www.biorb.com/

Hagen Aquatic Products:

Hagen Aquatic Products: Well-known manufacturer and maker of aquatic products including Powerheads and Canister Filters.

Web Site: www.hagen.com/usa/aquatic/

In the next issue:

Don't miss the next issue of the **"Tropical Fish Keeping Journal"** book edition five, featuring more products and in-depth features, for aquarists seeking a more successful and enjoyable tropical fish keeping experience.

Tropical Fish Keeping Journal Book Edition Five

In book edition five of the **"Tropical Fish Keeping Journal"** we cover; More about cures and remedies for fish diseases and with the avoidance of chemicals, to a specially prepared and created set of aquarists reference tables detailing aquarium sizes, filtration rates, heating requirements and sizes for aquariums, lighting wattage for fish tanks, biological culture volume mass, conversions and mathematical formulas for aquariums in litres, imperial US gallons and UK gallons, to identifying the different methods and techniques, surrounding tropical fish reproduction (breeding) and much more....

More details including aquarist readers news and updates from
The author's official web site:

http://www.alastairagutter.com

Printed in Great Britain
by Amazon

14032424R00071